My wife and I have been greatly helped by Justin's guidance and instruction. Finances are the largest stressor in our marriage, but by following through with Justin's counsel, we have been able to walk in unity, peace, and joy in this area. I am excited that more people will be helped through this book!

—**Matt Heerema**, Lead Pastor, Stonebrook Community Church

Finances are a significant worry for most of us. However, pretending it will just go away is taking foolishness to a new level. I truly appreciate Justin's intentional and developmental coach approach—his is not merely one more expert spewing information. Justin provides tangible steps for real growth and success.

—**John Robertson**, CEO and founder of FORTLOG Services, Inc.

If you're chained with debt, *Level Up Your Finances* is the key to long-term hope and freedom. Justin includes real-life stories that paint a clear picture of how living a "normal" financial life robs you of joy and keeps you from your goals. This book doesn't just include generic, one-size-fits-all financial advice. It's a blueprint to empower you to handle your financial situation.

—**Eric Snyder**, former president of Iowa State Police Association

Learning how to get a grip on our finances takes more than knowledge. And if anyone knows this, it's Justin Bennett. I'm not aware of a more passionate, caring financial coach. His clear and concise coaching process has helped thousands of clients—his Financial Freedom Pyramid Guide is brilliant! And by reading this book, you now have a personal coach, and Justin's wisdom in your hands. It takes time to right our financial ships. I promise, however, if you take that needed time, along with having a great coach in Justin Bennett to guide you along the way, you will successfully Level Up Your Finances.

—**Les Nienow**, Associate Director of Coaching, Ramsey Solutions

Simple, solid, practical, and understandable.

—**Steve Jones**, licensed mental health counselor, Executive Director, Cornerstone Counseling Center

This book is a beacon for anyone who has ever felt like they just can't get ahead. Justin provides practical tools and clear steps to achieve the financial freedom so many people long for.

—**Marianne Renner**, leadership coach, speaker, and author of *Self-Talk: 10 Stories You Tell Yourself That Hold You Back . . . And How to Overcome Them*

Level Up Your Finances is the real deal. Justin Bennett cuts through the noise and delivers a game plan that actually works . . . no fluff, no gimmicks, just real, actionable steps to take control of your money. His Financial Freedom Pyramid is a game-changer, providing a clear plan to eliminate debt, build wealth, and achieve financial freedom. If you're tired of stressing about money, living paycheck to paycheck, and feeling uncertain about your financial future, this book is for you. Read it, apply it, and watch your life transform.

—**Brandon Smith**, professional speaker, author, entrepreneur

I've read a lot of books on personal finances. Many of these by authors who were once, like Justin, drowning in debt and who turned things around to become debt-free and successful. So what makes this one different? For me, Justin's 5-step Financial Freedom Pyramid is the *best* explanation I've ever seen. The visual connected to the explanation is clear, simple to understand, and action-oriented, giving you something sticky to hold onto during your journey to Level Up Your Finances. This is an excellent book!

—**Kent Julian**, Certified Speaking Professional

Got money struggles? Read this book!!! If Justin has helped people pay off over ten million in debt, he's doing something right! Justin Bennett has written a thoroughly engaging, insightful, and heart-felt book that will give you hope . . . and the winning formula! Based on his own financial struggles with debt and those of his clients, you'll learn the path to financial stability and success Justin and his clients have achieved.

—**Kristine Stevenson**, EA, finance coach and author of *How to Avoid Trouble with the IRS: Ten Best Tax Tips for the Self-Employed, Gig Worker, and Indie Contractor*

LEVEL UP YOUR FINANCES

The name of the Lord is a strong tower;
the righteous run to it and are protected.

—Proverbs 18:10
(Christian Standard Bible)

LEVEL UP YOUR FINANCES

Say Goodbye to Winging It with Money

JUSTIN BENNETT

Strong Tower Press

Interior design: Gleniece Lytle, Desert Rain Editing
Graphic design: Jessica Bennett
Cover design: Lance Young
Photography: Kay Eileen Photography

CONTENTS

Phase Four: Momentum

Phase Five: Freedom

*To Jessica, my wife and best friend. I love you!
Without your steadfast encouragement and many hours of dedication
to this project, Level Up Your Finances would have never reached its
full potential. Your fingerprints are all over this book and from the
bottom of my heart, I thank you!*

*To our oldest son, Jacob, his wife, Rosa, and our granddaughter,
Autumn, our daughters, Jada, Julia, and Joelle, and our youngest son,
Josiah. You all mean the world to me! I am so grateful for your love and
support throughout this project.*

FOREWORD

LEVEL UP YOUR FINANCES is a practical book with a heart. That is because Justin Bennett is an author who cares deeply about helping people get out of their "money mess." Justin knows both the personal pain of feeling trapped in debt and the joyful freedom that goes with not owing any debt at all. He writes with a warm heart from the depth of his life experiences.

Justin hasn't just written good ideas that are unproven. He has developed a successful approach to help people get out of debt and into financial freedom. Some people write a book before they have the experience. Justin did the exact opposite, waiting until he truly had something to write about. When I read a book, I want to lean into the wisdom of someone who has proven experience and a track record of success. *Level Up Your Finances* is full of that proven and tested wisdom.

The best books on finances are insightful and enjoyable. *Level Up Your Finances* is both. Above all, this book is wildly practical. Every chapter offers clear steps to follow and gives concrete stories of individuals and couples that Justin has coached over the years. The clarity of this book makes it the best practical guide I have read on how to get out of debt.

As a pastor, I've watched Justin, and his wife, Jessica, live what they preach. I know Justin would be the first person to tell you he isn't perfect. But Justin and Jessica have implemented the tools they teach to others.

Their life and their joy are a testimony to the powerful reality that Justin's "Financial Freedom Pyramid" is a life changing tool.

Here's my advice: Get a copy of *Level Up Your Finances* for yourself. Carefully read through the wisdom in this book and consider how you can take your next step toward financial freedom. After that, go buy a second copy. Give it to a trusted friend and share how you want them to hold you accountable to the goals you have set. Have the courage to take your first step toward true financial freedom!

—Mark Vance, Lead Pastor
Cornerstone Church, Ames, IA

PREFACE

FINANCIAL FREEDOM AND FINANCIAL INDEPENDENCE are two phrases most people have heard of and want to achieve, but few have actually obtained either one. I define financial freedom as paying off all consumer debt and having a fully funded emergency fund of three to six months of living expenses.

If you take action on everything written about in this book, you will achieve financial freedom. This will allow you to save more money to invest for retirement, drive a nicer car, live in a nicer house, enjoy those vacations you have always dreamed of, and a whole lot more.

After crossing the finish line to financial freedom, the journey of building wealth and working towards financial independence begins. (Note: I do not cover financial independence in this book. Financial independence is where you have enough assets like investments or real estate to live the lifestyle you desire without having to work.) But is getting rich and building wealth all there is to financial independence?

You may not have heard of Truett Cathy, but chances are excellent you have heard about the restaurant chain he founded called Chick-fil-A. Cathy grew up dirt poor and was raised during the Great Depression. After all the success from his world-famous franchise, he died a multi-billionaire. Cathy's was a true rags to riches story.

Toward the end of his life, Cathy wrote a book called, *Wealth, Is It Worth it?* where he chronicled examples of wealth being a blessing or a curse for various people. The key difference was generosity. Being wealthy is not bad in and of itself; however, if your ultimate goal is to amass excessive wealth only for personal enjoyment and a sense of security, you'll be disappointed and ultimately realize wealth that focuses on oneself is meaningless.

Cathy proclaimed that wealth was completely worth it, but only if you were extremely generous. Throughout *Level Up Your Finances*, I use the Bible as a framework for good financial living. I understand that not every reader shares the same religious beliefs, and that's okay. I want to help everyone learn how to manage their finances well, while staying true to who I am.

An often quoted Bible passage with a strong warning is 1 Timothy 6:10: "For the love of money is the root of all kinds of evil, and by craving it, some have wandered away from the faith and pierced themselves with many pains."

However, later in verses 17 through 19, the apostle Paul told Timothy, "Instruct those who are rich in the present age not to be arrogant or to set their hope on the uncertainty of wealth, but on God, who richly provides us with all things to enjoy. Instruct them to do what is good, to be rich in good works, to be generous, willing to share, storing up for themselves a good reserve for the age to come, so that they may take hold of life that is real."

It's not wrong to make money. It's not wrong to build wealth. It's also not wrong to enjoy some of the money you have worked hard for. But it is good to be reminded that ultimately it's all God's, and if you keep that perspective and live generously, you'll be fulfilled, and, most importantly, you will fulfill a part of God's plan.

The Bible also says, "It is better to give than receive." But if you're deep in debt and don't have a solid financial foundation, it's challenging to be generous and impossible to be extremely generous. My goal, and the heart behind writing this book, is for you to first obtain financial freedom, which will lead you to financial independence and ultimately to being a generous giver.

INTRODUCTION

Perception Versus Reality

Success is not final, failure is not fatal: it is the courage to continue that counts.

—Winston Churchill

I WASN'T ALWAYS GOOD WITH MONEY. Even though I had a job in finance and a degree in business, I was like 78 percent of other Americans—living paycheck to paycheck.[1] By the third year of my marriage, covering the bills and essentials became impossible. Years of debt, careless spending, and terrible planning had dropped our checking and savings accounts to zero. In fact, we were almost $1,000 short every month, so we paid many of our bills with credit cards. We didn't know how to survive without debt!

My life on the surface looked like a typical family sitcom: pure domestic bliss with only a few minor problems. I had a beautiful family of five that would soon grow to seven, and our happy faces appeared on Christmas cards and in JCPenney portraits for everyone to see. We'd purchased our very first home when I was six years into my respectable banking career. It was a modest fixer upper we planned to turn a profit on after we'd made plenty of renovations and lasting memories. Wow! I was living the dream.

But my life wasn't even close to a casual, light-hearted family show. Every day, I was wracked with anxiety as I drove to my stable job and walked the halls of my promising house. There was a feeling of undeniable dread and fear that hung in the air around me like charged static electricity. I found myself asking, *Why am I feeling this way?* On a warm Midwestern day in June, I found out.

I wasn't sure why, but I sat down in my easy chair with a notebook, a pen, and a calculator. As someone who works in finance, these items help me figure out most problems, so it made sense to do it here. My plan was to write down everything going on in my head. Once I had it on paper, I'd be able to pat myself on the back and say, "See, it's all in your head, Justin. We're doing fine. You've just got a lot going on at work, and you haven't been eating well." However, when I totaled everything up, I realized what I felt wasn't because of a triple cheeseburger or a few overdue reports. I discovered we were $700 short every month! After paying all the bills and buying our necessities (not including things like Christmas, vacations, unexpected repairs, school supplies, or eating out), there was nearly a $1,000 deficit between what I earned and what we spent. This eye-opening situation was terrifying. So much for the picturesque all-American success story.

At first, I was in too much shock to feel the gravity of our problem. Instead of a gentle awakening that my finances were a mess, it hit me like a two-ton wrecking ball smashing into a Jenga tower. When I finally caught my breath and realized what I'd let happen, I was angry, sad, and totally humiliated. I worked in finance! How could we be in such a money mess, anyway? We didn't have expensive hobbies, shopping addictions, or even regular hankerings for lobster and fine wine.

You can probably identify with much of this scenario. Like many other people out there, I followed popular trends and random internet advice—which turned out to be unhelpful or downright bogus—and was blind to the fact that what I was doing with my money wasn't working. Being $700 in the hole clearly showed what I thought I knew about money management was baseless and faulty at best. But the first step to fixing a problem is realizing there is one. Believe me, I know what it's like to fail with money. Not only was I failing financially, but by default, I was failing my family and my career. I mean what kind of example was it that the finance guy was in debt? When my wife and I thought about our past, present, or future, all we could feel was dread and shame. It felt like we'd be stressing over bills and bracing for creditor calls for the rest of our lives. And long family vacations, entrepreneurial ventures, or dream homes?—ridiculous. I believed if I couldn't figure out how to fix my money problems on my own as someone who worked in finance, had a strong work ethic, and a pretty disciplined lifestyle, it was hopeless.

When the reality of your money situation sinks in as mine did on that June day, it can feel pretty hopeless too. Painful, overwhelming, like you're in too deep, and there's no way out. But guess what? I did get out. I didn't know it at the time, but that stressful revelation was the first step on my journey to living debt-free and becoming a financial coach who helps thousands of others live the same way. But how did I get into this money mess in the first place?

HOW DID I GET HERE?

Right after graduating high school, it was time to make my first big financial decision. What did I do? I got a credit card. I was told it was *the* way to build credit and stay prepared for emergencies. At the time it made sense, so I signed up. No harm, right? In fact, I was being "responsible" based on what everyone was telling me. Soon after that, like most people in my generation, I went to college. And like most people in my generation, I couldn't afford it. So, I did what everyone else was doing and signed up for student loans. While in college, my car was getting older, and again, everything I heard told me I needed a newer, more reliable car. Just like with the credit card, I thought I was being responsible. However, a "more reliable car" for me was code for "I want a newer, shinier toy," but I didn't have the courage to admit it. So, with no money and limited credit, I had someone cosign with me on a loan to purchase this car. Yes, you heard that right, I roped someone else into my mess.

Not long after I graduated from college, I began dating Jessica, the woman who would later become my wife. When it was time to propose, I was bound and determined not to get her a small diamond but had no money for a big, beautiful one. I believed she deserved that extravagant rock right now, not twenty years into the future, and in my wallet was that credit card with just enough available credit to buy an impressive and "respectable" ring for my soon-to-be wife. I swiped my trusty plastic friend and purchased the ring.

When I married my wife, she already had two kids from her previous marriage, and soon after we were expecting our first together. But we didn't have enough room in our cars for three kids, so we upgraded to an SUV. Again, we couldn't afford the upgrade, so we rolled over an old car loan on top of a new car loan and off we went. Off we went with a higher monthly car payment. Right after our daughter, Julia, was born, we decided to purchase our first home. It was soon after this that I found myself sitting in my recliner on that summer day realizing something was desperately wrong.

Everything up to that point in my life was seemingly by the book. I didn't think there was a reason to stress because no one told me I was doing anything wrong. In fact, everyone around me was making the same choices as I was making. When it hit me that we were in big financial trouble, this was all I could think about: If these were the best choices I could make in my early twenties, why was I so far in the hole? Why was I still living paycheck to paycheck? If all these money management techniques were correct, why was I still stressed and making no progress on my future money goals? Something wasn't right.

I know your situation feels confusing and frustrating because you're not a big spender, even if you have a few bad habits. You've never bought a luxury car. You don't regularly buy designer clothes or shoes. Your dinners aren't made by a private chef or served in a five-star restaurant. And you don't go to the salon weekly, let alone daily, for styling and manicures. Even if you've stumbled in a couple of these areas over the years, all-in-all, you'd probably say you're pretty economical and generally responsible with money, right? That was me too. We didn't go on half a dozen vacations a year, buy daily eight-dollar coffees, have memberships to expensive gyms, or splurge on fancy appliances. It felt like we were being so frugal, yet there was never any money leftover—I mean, there wasn't even enough to get through our monthly bills. Every day, there were more money problems, which I tried to solve using the standard methods. Basically, I asked the same people and referenced the same sources that helped me get into my money mess and looked to them to figure out how to get out of it. They'd always suggest things like balance transfers on credit cards, debt consolidation loans, and going back to school.

In fact, I tried all those methods. None of them worked. Every year, I would do balance transfers to keep my credit card interest rate at zero percent. However, the balances year after year kept growing. We eventually took out a debt consolidation loan to reduce our monthly payment and to pay fewer bills every month. In order to do that, we had to use our house as collateral and get a second mortgage. Now our house was at a much greater risk of foreclosure. My last attempt to get our finances in order using what I learned from society was to go back to school. With no money to pay for it, we borrowed more on top of the student loans I already had. Did you catch that? To fix my money problems, I raised my home and student loan debt and monthly payments. Tell me how that makes any sense.

HOW DID WE GET OUT?

The internet boasts a hundred ways to get out of debt from the avalanche method to house hacking to vending machine hustles. Some are practical. Some are wild. Most don't work. Fortunately, my wife and I found Financial Peace University[2] and were able to pay off over $100,000 of debt using Dave Ramsey's Baby Steps.[3] With all our debt gone and our emergency fund in place, we now enjoy financial freedom. We have the margin in our finances to take our kids on fun experiences without going into debt. We have the savings to fix our cars or appliances when they break. We have abundance to give freely and joyfully to the church, local non-profits, and other causes that are near and dear to our hearts. When I sit back and recall all the sacrifices we made to clean up our financial mess—it was all worth it.

What we learned from Ramsey's guidance changed our lives as well as millions of others. His principles are backed by multiple studies and by hundreds of thousands of testimonies. But this is not a book about Dave Ramsey or a rehash of his methods. I wouldn't be surprised if you're rolling your eyes reading Dave Ramsey's name, ready to shut the book and accept your money situation as it is. But hold tight. I see you. You tried Financial Peace University along with everything else, and it didn't work either, right? You didn't see the results everyone boasts about in their debt-free screams. In fact, those screams on the podcast make you want to give up. Each one is a reminder that you don't have what it takes to win with your money.

When I opened my financial coaching business to help others using the Ramsey method, I realized almost all my clients were in your position. Sick and tired of their situation but unable to get results. The problem you and many others are facing needs a specific approach that addresses more than knowledge—you need accountability. There's a disconnect between your head knowledge and your behavior, meaning you know *what* to do, but can't make it work. You can't change your habits, though you've tried again and again. Or, you're doing what the plan says, but there's not enough money to pay off your overwhelming debt, and you want to give up. Whoever you are—please don't.

After nearly two decades of coaching thousands of households to go from failure to freedom with their finances, there's no doubt in my mind you can reach your goals and stop living from one tight paycheck to the next. Years of failing and struggling with money can weigh down a person so heavily it also destroys other things they care about like relationships, hobbies, careers, and future ambitions. You can leave those feelings of dread, fear, and shame behind and finally live in peace. I've coached many people like you, people who initially walked through my door or joined my online sessions with their heads hung low, feeling overwhelmed and exhausted over the magnitude of their situation, to finally breathe sighs of relief and live stress-free.

Why is it that money is a taboo subject, making so many people tackle their money problems on their own rather than getting help? It takes people two to four years to reach out to me after they hear about my services.

(It took one guy ten years!) But after the first month, they almost always say, "Why didn't I do this sooner?" and by the sixth month working with me, my clients pay off an average of $10,000 to $20,000 in debt. I'm here to tell you there is hope.

You don't have to be good at math to get out of debt. You don't need a history of being disciplined and reaching goals. You don't even need to earn a certain income. I've worked with everyone, from Masters in Business Administration holders to retail clerks, business leaders to single parents. I even helped a couple (with nine children!) get out of debt who were short $4,000 a month. Every situation was different, but the missing piece for all of them was the same—lack of accountability. Few people realize this is their biggest hurdle, so they spin their wheels forever and gain no traction, accept their failure, and give up on their dream of financial freedom. As your financial coach, I will show you what's possible, give you the tools you need, and motivate you so you have the power to achieve your dream. Truly, no matter your circumstances, you can find financial freedom and restore your hope for a prosperous and peaceful future.

Financial Freedom
Pyramid Guide

I BECAME A FINANCIAL COACH to help people like myself who have repeatedly failed with their money and desperately want a way out of the mess, but the standard formula hasn't gotten them closer to their dream of financial freedom. Over the years, I've refined a solution that's helped thousands of clients pay off a total of over ten million dollars in debt by developing a system for getting out of debt and reaching your goals. I call this the Financial Freedom Pyramid. This five-level plan bridges the gap between where you are now and where you want to be—at peace at the pinnacle of the Pyramid. What this plan doesn't do is simply give you a few helpful tips about money rooted in trends and half-truths, while expecting you to apply them all seamlessly and achieve an idyllic photo finish. No. The Financial Freedom Pyramid is backed by proven principles, and what you gain from each level builds onto the next as your hope climbs. Awareness leads to clarity, Knowledge to understanding, Commitment to results, Momentum to traction, and lastly, Freedom to peace with your finances.

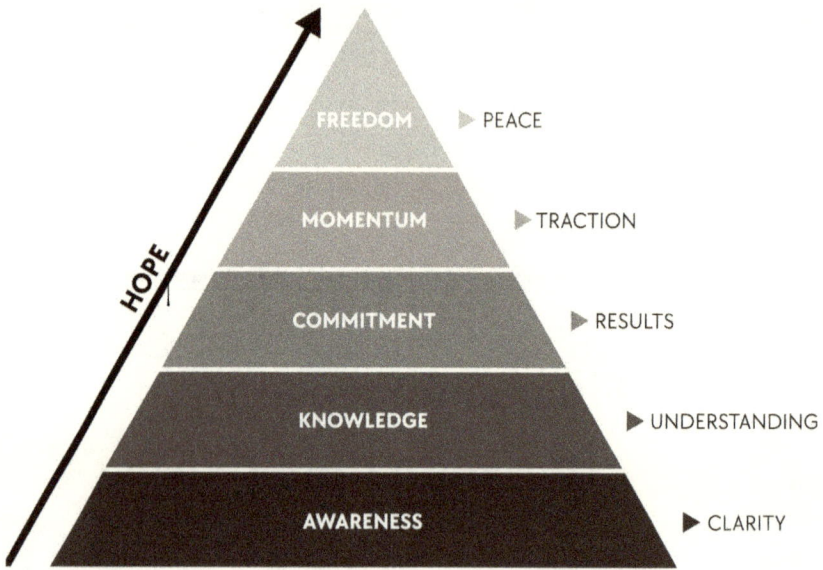

AWARENESS

Level One is where you stop guessing and start knowing exactly where you stand with your money. This is where you're going to find out exactly what your financial goals are, what your income and expenses are, and how much debt you're in. Here, you stop guessing and end the feeble attempts at doing it all in your head. Say good-bye to winging it with your finances. At the end of the Awareness Level, you will have gained clarity. This is important because when you get organized, the steps to financial freedom get a whole lot clearer.

KNOWLEDGE

On Level Two, you're fully aware of your financial state, so now you need to learn the how-tos of financial success. I'm talking about the initial foundations of personal finance: budgeting, saving, and getting out of debt. What I've discovered is that it's next to impossible to live the life you want and be at peace when you have no budget, no savings, and a pile of debt. Learning these basic principles on the Knowledge Level will lead you to a greater understanding of your messy situation and how to get out of it.

COMMITMENT

Level Three is your fork-in-the-road moment. If you say yes to what you learn on the Knowledge level, you'll see results after each paycheck. Making a commitment is the easy part. It's living out the commitment that's the challenging part. On the Commitment Level, you'll learn what it takes to stay committed, break free from the Cycle of Regret (more about this in Chapter 8), and be well on your way to experiencing the financial freedom you've only dreamed about.

MOMENTUM

On Level Four, the results you achieve every month will lead you to the traction you've always been looking for. You'll finally be motivated to conquer anything that lies ahead. However, if you're not careful during the Momentum Level, one of the four thieves might S.L.O.W. you down and threaten the traction you've gained. We will discuss how to overcome these four thieves in Chapter 11.

FREEDOM

Lastly, I'll see you at the top of the Pyramid on Level Five. Here, you're living on a budget with confidence. You've paid off all your debt but your house and have a fully funded emergency savings of three to six months of living expenses. On the Freedom Level, you're no longer in financial bondage but can now choose what to do with your money. You have a sense of peace with your finances like never before.

However, getting control of finances is kind of like dieting. You know what you need to do, but you just can't make yourself stick to it. Or you convince yourself it's a problem with the plan, and you try one plan after another only to find they're equally difficult. Then, defeated, you give up. I call this the Cycle of Regret. It goes like this:

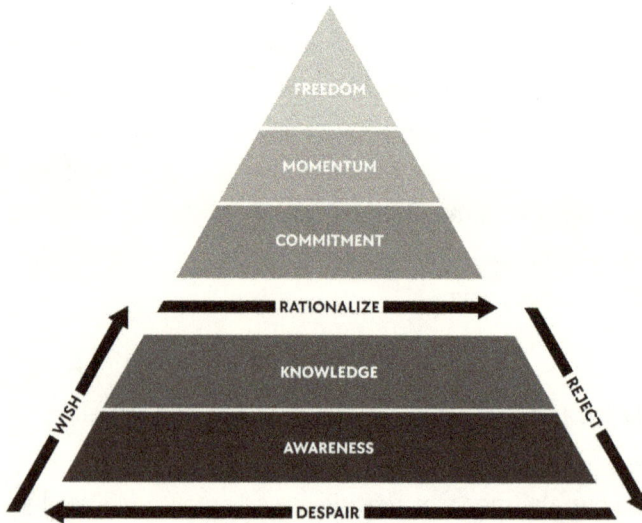

CYCLE OF REGRET

You wish for your new plan to work. You have high hopes that it will. But soon after you start, you rationalize and make exceptions on a rule here or a rule there. After a while, you make more and more compromises, rejecting what you have learned, and you find yourself in despair over your lack of discipline and progress. Finally, you accept your failure and deep regret follows. You don't do anything for a while, but eventually, you pick up a new plan, start the cycle again, only to end up going nowhere.

So, how do you bridge the gap between knowledge and commitment and avoid returning to the Cycle of Regret? Accountability. As a financial coach, I've discovered people need accountability either (1) to start, (2) to finish, or (3) from start to finish.

This doesn't just apply to finances either. It could be fitness goals, nutrition goals, career goals—anything. But in terms of money, account-ability to get started means you need someone to be there while you're getting the hang of your budget or paying off your first few debts. After that, you'll have enough momentum to finish it on your own. Accountability to finish means you need someone to be there toward the end of your new financial plans so you don't get complacent and permit yourself to fall back into old ways. An accountability partner or coach will keep you focused until the end. And if you need accountability from start to finish because it's all hard, that's okay. Everyone needs a coach, whether it's for one time or for a lifetime.

THIS BOOK

Throughout this book, I will be that coach. *Level Up Your Finances* is not a book about investments or wealth-building, but about how to build your financial foundation to later build wealth upon. It's more than a personal finance how-to, it's a live coaching session, adaptable and informative whether you have six figures of debt or minimal amounts of debt. I'll take you through the same process I followed to fix my financial mistakes, the same process my clients followed that fixed theirs, and help you out of the Cycle of Regret that's held you back. I'll provide you with the tools you need to destroy your debt, build your savings, and develop healthy money habits. Will it take the whole book to get there? Yes. There's no quick-fix or secret hack that's going to get you to your goals. (If there were, you'd have found it already.) It took a while to get into your money mess, and it'll take a while to get out. Each level of the Pyramid is a steady, guided process, not a quick escalator ride to the top. Remember, the pace is important for success.

I want to help you create a reality you didn't think was possible. Why settle for being free of credit-card debt when you can pay off the house early? Why be content not living paycheck to paycheck when you can have thousands in savings? Why accept a life where you can afford to eat out once a week when you can have that *and* take that fourteen-day dream vacation to Jamaica? It's time to scale the Pyramid to learn how. Each part of this book, from meaningful statistics and essential habits to motivating success stories and eye-opening exercises (a detailed checklist is included in the back of the book), is filled with wisdom and hope and will stair-step you from your current place of despair and shame to a landing with a view of your future financial prosperity.

Life is too short to be broke and live scared. Take this journey with me. Freedom is just around the corner . . . Let's go!

LEVEL ONE

Awareness

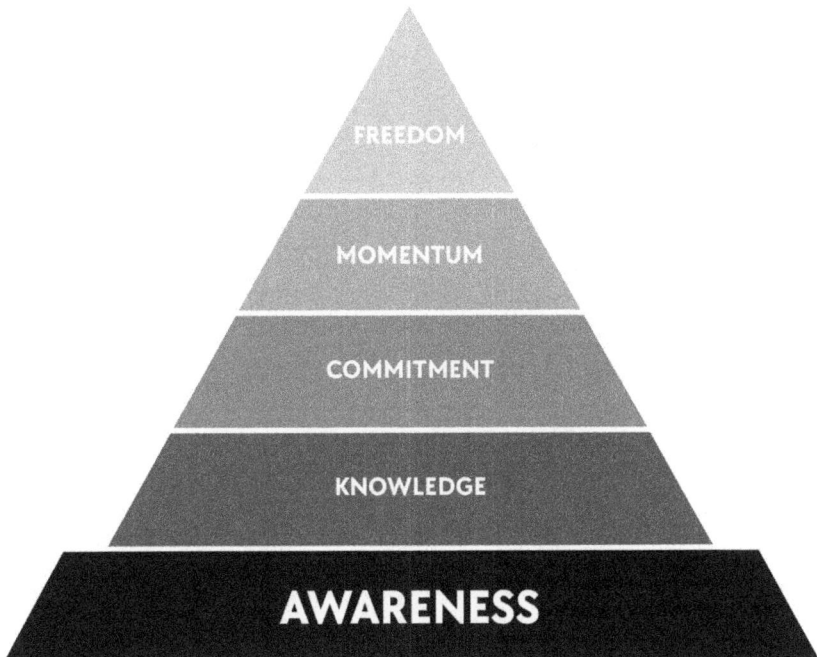

CHAPTER 1

Turn On the Lights

We cannot solve our problems with the same thinking we used when we created them.

—Albert Einstein

"YOU KNOW . . . I REALLY DON'T LIKE people like you and Dave Ramsey," a man said to me after I finished a talk on personal finance at a conference. It was rare that anyone came up to me after a presentation and insulted me—actually, I don't think it'd ever happened before. Most of the time, people are thanking me and asking follow-up questions; however, this gentleman was clearly not impressed by my budgeting advice. But I bounced back and said, "Thank you for coming today. How can I help you?"

He scoffed and said, "Whenever *I* do a budget, it says my wife and I have $600 left over every month, but we never see it!" The attendee obviously thought he caught me in a real gotcha moment. What he didn't know was that I heard stories like his every day. "If you're struggling to make your budget work," I said, "you and your wife should sign up for financial coaching."

Somehow, that invitation (or was it a challenge?) spurred him to do just that. I'm guessing he was looking for a way to trap me in some elaborate personal finance hoax. Whatever the reason, I was more than happy to meet with him and his wife. I have had plenty of people start my coaching sessions with a negative attitude, but they almost always come around as we work through the Financial Freedom Pyramid.

When I met with the couple for their first session, I asked where they'd rank their emotions about their current financial situation on a scale of 1–10. (One meaning so stressed and anxious you can't think straight. Ten meaning perfectly at peace and content.) They gave me a *three*! There were tears streaming down his wife's face when she told me, "Justin, we are so stressed with money. I check my bank accounts online every day to make sure I don't have any overdraft fees. I am constantly moving money from account to account to avoid overdrafts. I am sick and tired of living this way! We will do anything within legal and moral bounds to fix our situation. Please, help us get out of this mess!"

A COMMON TALE

This wasn't the first couple to come into my office completely overwhelmed and swallowed by their financial situation. A majority of the country is strapped for cash, living paycheck to paycheck, and under constant financial stress.[1] In fact, Americans owe just under eighteen trillion dollars of consumer debt![2] Even if you're paying your bills each month, you still feel trapped with no wiggle room for emergencies or expenses like car repairs, medical bills, and home maintenance needs that you know are coming but pray will happen another day. If you can't cover these unexpected expenses, you've got a big problem.

Also, do you realize all we've talked about is the present? You're probably getting up every day only focused on surviving the next twenty-four hours. You're like someone lost in the woods. Getting out of the forest is important, but it doesn't take priority over finding food, water, and shelter before dark. My guess is that long-term financial security is entirely off your radar as nearly half of the country has no money for retirement and is swimming, or should I say, drowning in debt.[3] Your debt is one of the main reasons you feel like you can't win with money despite all your efforts.

Forty-seven percent of people living in America carry over credit card balances from month to month,[4] and many of them have significant student loans between $35,000–$50,000 on average.[5] Car loans have become so normal many people don't even categorize them as debt in their minds, but that huge payment due every month is a significant reminder of that big hole Americans have dug themselves into. The average car payment is between $600–$700 a month.[6] (It wasn't that long ago that $700 was the average mortgage payment!) But the amount really doesn't matter. Despite what anyone has told you, all debt is bad. A fifteen-year home mortgage (as opposed to a thirty-year mortgage that will cost you hundreds of thousands more in interest) should be the only debt you consider, and all other debt is damaging to your financial future.

I understand this message is counterculture. I also understand that a lot of the information I present will be the opposite of what society tells you, but my research and experience together make me certain that living debt-free is the key to breaking free from money's hold over your life. Financial freedom starts when you don't owe anyone anything and all your income is yours.

This idea of living debt-free may sound crazy. After all, it's not really what you hear about on TV and on podcasts—plus, everyone has debt, right? But before we climb aboard the what-everyone-else-does train, ask yourself why you are here. Why are you sitting here reading this book? Aren't you here because what's normal and widely accepted isn't working? Despite following the advice of your favorite money-savvy TikToker or TV personality, you're still broke, stressed, and behind where you want to be. Obviously, something's broken, and doing it the "usual way" isn't going to cut it. This is why the Awareness Level is so essential. You must understand how the systems we've identified as standard and typical are far from healthy or helpful.

On the next level of the Pyramid, we'll get into the right and wrong ways to handle money, but the point is you need to remember it was the "normal" advice and the "normal" consumer behavior that got you into your financial mess. What you think you know about personal finance simply doesn't work with practical application. Once you become aware of this, we can break everything back down to the foundation and rebuild stronger and smarter money habits. Starting on the Awareness Level, we need to examine where you are with your money today, that way you can start running from your present pain and toward a much brighter future with clarity and hope. Time to get out a notebook, pen, and calculator. We have work to do.

WHAT'S HAPPENING IN YOUR HOUSE?

The state of American personal finance is concerning. Actually, it's a total mess. Like the couple from the beginning of this chapter, the average person's financial reality is worse than they think, so I want to zoom in and reveal what a budget would look like for the average American. Since we're at the Awareness Level of your journey, it makes sense that I help you get a full picture of your financial situation. There may be parts of your budget that are better or worse than the average American, but you can't move forward with a solid plan without a good idea of where you are right now.

The sample budget below is based on what the average American family of four spends in these categories, and though it may not reflect your spending exactly, it should give you a window into your current situation.

AVERAGE HOUSEHOLD BUDGET

Item	Amount	Item	Amount
Income (after Taxes)[7]	$5,353	Credit Card Payments[14]	$272
Mortgage[8]	$2,201	Utilities[15]	$329
Food[9]	$1,306	Cell Phone[16]	$157
Clothing[10]	$162	Internet[17]	$89
Fuel[11]	$179	Car Insurance[18]	$212
Car Payments[12]	$690	Subscriptions[19]	$219
Student Loan[13]	$307	Income – Expenses	– $770

Does this budget seem about right to you? Well, there's one problem—it's in the red! There's a $770 per month deficit in this budget that is keeping the average American, and probably you, in debt and in the drowning paycheck-to-paycheck lifestyle, which does not include things like eating out, car registrations, pet expenses, kids activities, personal care, and medical expenses.

BUDGET TOTAL

Income (after Taxes)	–	Expenses	=	Total
$5,353	–	$6,123	=	– $770

The U.S. Bureau of Labor Statistics agrees, estimating the average American household spends $6,081 per month. If the average after-tax income is $5,353, that leaves the typical American household short $728 per month.[20] This is where my wife and I were—$700 short every month. But we got out of it and you can too.

This would be a good time to write down your income and expenses or whip out whatever you have for a budget to see if your monthly expenses exceed what you bring in each month. Even if your budget doesn't look exactly like the sample, the principle is the same. You're likely in debt with little savings and barely enough to get by. I'm sure right about now as you look at what you wrote down, your face is getting hot, and your heart is beating fast. Just breathe! This feeling isn't forever, and we can get through it. The financial tools you've been using to go about your day-to-day life are the wrong tools and ruining your chances for financial freedom. With a reset, you'll be on your way out of despair and on to hope.

WE'RE NOT USING THE SAME MEASURING STICK

I have some clients who say, "Well, I'm not doing *too* bad." After they tell me something like this, the client goes on to explain that their debts are lower than the norm, they have a slightly older car than their friends do, and they don't eat out all the time like their co-workers. Proclaiming their situation isn't "too bad" brings a lot of comfort to my clients, but it's really a defense mechanism they use to avoid despair. If your financial circumstances are better than someone else's, but you're still living paycheck to paycheck, you're setting the bar way too low for yourself. As you will learn in Chapter 2, you don't have enough pain to want the relief!

You shouldn't measure your financial success by the worst examples around you; you should look at the best. Otherwise, you'll be limiting your potential and giving yourself permission to continue making big financial mistakes. Sure, maybe someone else's money mistake costs them $10,000 and yours only costs you $2,000. But that's still lost potential that could have helped you become a future millionaire (or at least helped you dig yourself out of debt).

Ask yourself what is your model for personal finances. This is important, because where we form our money principles needs to come from a trusted source. Unfortunately, many of us weren't taught about money in school, and maybe our parents kept their own affairs private, so our model might be a friend, a family member, or some social media influencer. However, with these examples, you can't be certain you're getting the whole picture, and their advice may or may not be backed by real data and success stories outside their own. They could even be lying to you about their financial mess (out of embarrassment more than malice), but if you're following their lead, you'll probably end up in the same sticky situation.

HOW ARE YOU FEELING NOW?

I ask all my clients in our first session together how they feel about their current financial situation on a 1–10 scale to better help me understand their level of shame, panic, or despair. Their answer helps me gauge how motivated they are to achieve their goals and how big the emotional release will be when they finally get there. That last part is important because the vice-like grip of debt can impact you so emotionally it erodes your mental health, your relationships, and anything that could make you happy.

EMOTION SCALE

1	2	3	4	5	6	7	8	9	10

Hopeless - Overwhelmed - Stressed - Hopeful - Confident - Peaceful

Where do you see yourself on this scale? As you go through the Pyramid, I want you to come back and rate yourself again. I want you to remember how you felt at the beginning of your journey, and realize how much has changed as you progress up the Pyramid.

That couple at the beginning of the chapter rated themselves very low in their first session, and the wife was crying and begging me to help her family. I'm happy to report that six months later, the couple informed me their number three had turned into a nine. The wife was still crying, but this time it was tears of joy! They had paid off thousands of dollars in debt and paid $3,000 in cash for unplanned expenses in our time together. The wife also told me, "Justin, do you remember when we first started working together, I was getting paid weekly?" I told her I did. "Do you also remember that after a couple months of working with you, I went from getting paid once a week to getting paid every other week?"

"Yes," I said, giving her a quizzical look and laughing a little. "What's the point you're trying to make?"

"Justin! We went from getting paid weekly to biweekly. We went a whole week without pay. If you would have told me six months ago that I could have gone without pay for a week and remained totally stress-free, I would have asked you what you were smoking, and would you share some please?"

It sounds like such a small thing, but this was everything to her. Though they'd paid off thousands at this point, they still had a long way to go, but it was clear to them after a few sessions that the plan was working, and with that came a ton of much-needed relief and motivation. They didn't need to cross the finish line to get to that nine, they just needed to know the finish line was there. You don't need to complete all your goals to feel relief from your pain. Peace with your money is much closer than you think. You'll suddenly complete a task you never thought you could, and it'll feel great! But the first step to getting control of your finances is turning on the lights in your financial house and looking at what's really going on. You need to see the depth of your debt and the hurdles of your current lifestyle before we can make a plan and move forward.

To do this, I need you to begin tracking all your expenses for the next thirty days (feel free to use any tool that works for you: a notebook, a notes app, or spreadsheet). I also want you to pull out the last couple pay stubs and see what your gross pay versus your take-home pay is. See how much your deductions and benefits (like health or disability insurance) are costing you. In this Awareness Level exercise, understand there's no shame. You need to determine what you're spending on everything right now and zero in on your specific circumstances. I had one client after the first ten days of this exercise say, "I can tell you why I'm broke—Starbucks! Every day was Starbucks ... six bucks. Starbucks ... six bucks. Starbucks ... six bucks." Like my client did in the example below, when you keep track of all your expenses, you'll finally become aware of where all your money is *really* going.

EXPENSE TRACKER

Date	Payment To	Description	Paid With	Amount
9/16	Aldi	Groceries	Debit Card	$288.53
9/16	Starbucks	Coffee	Cash	$6.13
9/16	Shell	Gas	Credit Card	$44.00
9/17	City Water	Utilities	Online	$72.99
9/17	Starbucks	Coffee	Cash	$6.13
9/18	Starbucks	Coffee	Cash	$6.13
9/18	Mechanic	Car Repair	Credit Card	$548.32

And since you are turning on all the lights, also take a moment to list all the debt you have. You will want to include who you owe the money to, what is the total balance owed, minimum monthly payment required, due date, and interest rate. If you haven't logged into your accounts in a while, you may need to reset some passwords. All the numbers you are collecting will be organized in Chapter 6 when I walk you through a step-by-step process to create your first budget.

There's no mess too big to clean up. There is no dumb choice I haven't seen before—honestly, there are probably few dumb choices I haven't made myself! Put every expense down in your chosen tool and don't estimate. Don't worry about making any adjustments or balancing your budget right now. The purpose of this exercise is purely to help you become aware of where all your spending is truly going. You'll find some spending habits that you'll be pleasantly surprised weren't as bad as you thought. And you'll find some spending habits that will shock you on how much you're really spending.

No matter what your spending looks like and how far you're in the hole, you should be incredibly proud of yourself for taking this first step. Awareness is essential for clarity and clarity is essential for knowledge. After knowledge, you'll have a clear understanding of what you need to do, and with commitment to my plan, you'll see big results that will drive you all the way to the top of the Pyramid. Let's continue!

Chapter 1 Takeaways

- **Freedom starts when you don't owe anyone anything and all your income is yours.** Living debt-free is the key to breaking free from money's hold over your life.

- **Rank how you feel about your money situation from one to ten.** Evaluate your emotional progress by asking yourself where you are on the emotion scale at least once every three months.

- **Peace with your money is much closer than you think.** You don't need to complete all your goals to feel relief from your pain. The first step to getting control of your finances is seeing the depth of your debt and the hurdles of your current lifestyle before you make a plan and move forward.

- **Track all your income and expenses for thirty days.** Track everything you spend whether it is a bill, groceries, one-time expense, debt payment, etc. Whether you use a debit card, credit card, cash, or Venmo, it doesn't matter. Every penny that you spend needs to be tracked. Also, review your pay stubs to see how much is being taken out for deductions, benefits, etc.

- **Document all of your debt.** Write down who each of your creditors are, how much you owe, how much your minimum monthly payments are, and the interest rate for each debt.

CHAPTER 2

Begin with the End

To begin with the end in mind means to start with a clear understanding of your destination.

—*Stephen R. Covey,*
The 7 Habits of Highly Effective People

IF YOU TOOK A ROAD TRIP but didn't know where you were headed, you'd feel lost. But if you're heading toward a destination you've always dreamed about, the drive, though long, would be exhilarating and joyful because you couldn't wait to get there. Our financial journeys are the same way. Even if you're following a research-backed plan, it won't matter if you don't know where you're going. Stephen Covey's quote is good advice; however, for most people who've tried and failed getting ahead with their money, the idea of dreaming of an idyllic end destination can be challenging, if not downright impossible. Why is that?

When it comes to people's finances, it can be hard to see past the next paycheck. Bill after bill comes due. Setback after setback comes out of nowhere (and have you ever noticed setbacks usually come in threes?), and these setbacks usually come right about the time they're getting some traction with their money. Because this is so discouraging, they throw up their hands and give up. Sure, they know they should be saving for retirement and other future goals, but when they have little to nothing in savings, a pile of debt, and are living in bondage paycheck to paycheck, it seems like a worthless exercise to think about their exhilarating and joyful end of their financial journey.

So for me to ask you to begin with the end may seem futile. But when you see your end goals as a reality and not as hopeless wishes, this fuels you to start on the path of financial freedom like nothing else will.

START BY SETTING GOALS

Earl Nightingale says, "If a person is working toward a predetermined goal and knows where to go, then that person is successful."[1] What I have discovered is if you set short-term present goals, it becomes much easier to think about future goals. The first thing I have my clients do is determine where they want to go by writing down their short-term goals. I define short-term goals as any goal you want to accomplish in the next three to six months. Below is a typical sample of short-term goals.

Short-Term Goals (three to six months)
- Stop living paycheck to paycheck
- Start an emergency fund
- Pay down debt
- No longer encounter overdraft fees
- Eliminate all credit cards
- Be more disciplined with budgeting
- Be on the same page with your spouse

Next, I have my clients determine what long-term goals they want to achieve. These goals are long range goals, anywhere from six months to a year from now all the way to the end of their life and beyond to the next generation. Below is a typical sample of long-term goals.

Long-Term Goals (more than six months)
- Pay off all consumer debt
- Establish a fully-funded emergency fund
- Purchase a home
- Invest towards retirement
- Increase generosity
- Pursue a dream career or business
- Go on annual vacations
- Renovate your house
- Pay off your house early
- Purchase investment property
- Enjoy retirement
- Create a secure legacy for your children

WHAT IS YOUR WHY?

Once we've established both short- and long-term goals, I ask my clients to take it a step further. Under each goal, I want to know why that goal is important to them. Your goals must have strong *whys* if you're serious about wanting to achieve them. The answer to why you're doing this will push you to stay with the plan even when the going gets tough. With a deeper understanding of your why in mind, you'll be able to picture your idyllic future and know it's not a dream, but something possible—something to hope for!

Before we move any further onto the Awareness Level, let's go over these three important points:

1. **You must own your goals.** As your coach, I want to know what's important to you. These are your goals, not mine.
2. **Write down your goals.** Written goals have a much better chance of succeeding—a 42 percent higher chance—than not writing them down.[2]

3. **You must have a strong why.** Public speaker Jim Rohn said, "When the why is strong, the how becomes easy" and "The bigger the why, the easier the how."[3]

Own your goals

If you ask a coach in any field, we'd all say the same thing: We cannot want the end results more than our clients. When I first started coaching, I discovered when I wanted their goal more than they did, both my client and I would be frustrated and their results would be minimal at best.

I tell my prospective clients they need two things besides their income to help them achieve their goals: (1) They have to be sick and tired of their situation, and (2) they have to be teachable. That doesn't mean they become a floor mat while I dictate how they live their financial lives. It means they're willing to learn something new or willing to apply something they've attempted in the past but from a different perspective. Now, let me ask you: Are you sick and tired of your situation? Are you teachable? If your answer is yes to these questions, then stick with me. I'm here to help you reach your goals. Is it hard? . . . yes. Is it worth it? . . . absolutely!

Write down your goals

It doesn't matter if you write down your goals in a journal, a document on your computer, or on a phone app. Any goal in any area of your life should be written down, and your financial goals are no exception. Author Michael Hyatt offers five reasons why your goals need to be in writing.[4] When your goals are written down, they will:

1. Force you to clarify what you want
2. Motivate you to take action
3. Provide a filter for other opportunities
4. Help you overcome resistance
5. Enable you to see—and celebrate—your progress

He also went on to say, "Life is hard. It's particularly difficult when you aren't seeing progress. You feel like you are working yourself to death and going nowhere. But written goals are like mile markers on a highway. They enable you to see how far you've come and how far you need to go. They also provide an opportunity for celebration when you get there."

If you are looking for a simple way to give yourself the best chance to obtain financial freedom, you *must* write down your goals. And if you want to more than double your chances in reaching your goals, find someone to hold you accountable to them. We will discuss this more fully in Chapter 9.

Have a strong *why*

Let me ask you some questions. Why do all this? Why change your situation? Why buckle down and commit to a budget? Why waste time reading personal finance books? Why bring a coach or friend along to keep you accountable? How embarrassing! Why do any of this?

The reality is if your why isn't big enough, no amount of awareness or knowledge will get you anywhere. Dr. Phil once said, "Awareness without action is worthless."[5] Well, isn't that the truth! It makes me think of a story I heard recently about a child bitten by a deadly, venomous spider. The antivenom needed for the child wasn't legal in the US, so the boy's father traveled to Mexico and smuggled the medicine back into the country to save his child. This was a law-abiding citizen who never in his worst nightmares thought he would be involved in a criminal act like this, but he had a very strong *why* and that powered him to do the impossible. (The child survived, and the father did not go to jail, for anyone on the edge of their seat.)

Now this example is obviously extreme. No one is dying here! And I am definitely not suggesting you do anything illegal. However, we need something that ignites the same drive and vigor. Because if you want that end goal badly enough, you'll feel like nothing can stop you. Most importantly, you'll finally realize the pain that your inaction causes you is greater than the pain of taking action on your goals. And you need to feel that if you want to reach your target.

FINDING AND DEFINING YOUR WHY

Think about all the things you want for your life that don't seem attainable yet. Envision that trip to the Maldives with your toes buried in the warm sand and the scent of salt water in the air. Picture cooking Thanksgiving dinner in that remodeled kitchen with the eight-burner gas stove. Imagine funding the youth group's entire mission trip. Or simply think about sitting on your front porch in peace, with no chaotic, anxiety-filled thoughts about incoming bills, looming debt, and unstable savings. Imagine having the funds to live like you want and give like you want without stress.

One of the most memorable experiences I've had as a financial coach was when I pressed my client to define his why. He wanted to get out of debt. Okay. But *why*, I asked. What was the vision of the future he had that couldn't be reached without first getting out of debt? He sheepishly told me he wanted to change careers. It was clear he thought changing careers was no more than a pipe dream and was embarrassed to tell me about it. After a little prompting, he admitted he wanted to be a bookbinder. Now that was a new one for me! I heard travel, adoption, entrepreneurship, muscle cars, and so much more, but never a bookbinder. I had no idea that this was still a current job title, and I definitely didn't think anyone would aspire to be one.

After a little more digging, he actually started to cry. He told me his grandfather was a bookbinder, and when he was young, they'd spend the weekends gushing over old books and stitching back together these antique, collectible volumes of classic stories. He loved spending that time with his grandfather, and it always inspired him when they brought new life to those old books and joy to their collectors. My client wanted to get out of debt to connect with his past and bring joy back to his present.

No matter your age or situation, we can get you to your dream, even if it's a little unusual. It's not too late to turn your life around, win with your money, and make your dreams a reality, not just hopes you've written in a journal. Believe this future is possible because your path to financial freedom depends on it. If you haven't already, take a moment to define your short- and long-term goals. Dream about the future you never thought you could have. Then write down each goal and ask yourself why is this goal important to you—just like my bookbinder client. Author and podcaster Ken Coleman says, "If your *why* does not make you cry, it is not your *why*."[6]

LEAVE YOUR PRESENT PAIN

Years ago, I remember hearing about an intriguing experiment. Groups of new car salesmen at some high-end sports car company were given two different incentives. The first group was told that if they sold ten cars in three months, they'd get their own luxury sports car completely free. Sounds like a good deal, right? It's definitely motivating. The second group was given a car on the very first day and told if they didn't sell ten cars in three months, the company would take the car back. Ouch! That definitely would put some fire under your butt.

So, which had the better result? The people threatened with losing their shiny new sports cars were more successful. Why? Because humans are more willing to move away from pain than move toward comfort. A small amount of discomfort will motivate us to get going, but it takes a pretty significant and tangible prize to drive us toward a pleasant result. This is an unfortunate reality, but you need to be aware of your human nature in order to get through the five levels of the Financial Freedom Pyramid.

Given this information, keep your long-term goals in the back of your mind, but let's examine how you may be feeling right now. You're in pain, and you want it to stop so you can get to a place of comfort and joy. When you think about all the emotions that come with earning, spending, and saving money, I'm sure most of it is not positive. It's more like your hand is touching a hot stove and you absolutely need to make a change to stop the burning.

When your finances aren't in order, the ambient stress affects everything you do. There's no getting around it. Before I sat down with my notebook, pen, and calculator all those years ago, I felt tense and suffocated all the time but didn't know why. When I became fully aware of my situation, the stress and despair got worse because I didn't know how to get out of the mess. Money, in some way, is related to everything we do in life, so when we don't handle it well, the consequence of that choice radiates through every part of our lives. We can't enjoy a vacation or stay present at our children's birthday parties. We can't take a day off for sickness or book appointments without stress. And we're always bracing for that inevitable notification that our accounts have hit zero dollars or there's "insufficient funds" to complete a transaction. Some of us even feel physical effects like migraines and muscle soreness. Money can grip our whole lives—especially when it's out of control.

Furthermore, we've only discussed the emotional side of things. There are tangible threats, too, like foreclosure, bankruptcy, repossession, wage garnishment and more. So, in order to move forward, you need to become fully aware of your present pain. Just like those sports car salesmen, this pain will help motivate you to stay on your path to financial freedom. It's also a great reminder of the relief you'll feel well before you reach your destination. If highlighting all this pain is overwhelming and triggering, I get it, but be encouraged.

As you go through the Awareness Level, you'll feel relief almost immediately because the ugly money mess you shoved under the bed is now laid out in front of you, and it's not as scary as you thought. Awareness brings clarity, remember? And that clarity brings you that much closer to your goals. Not close enough to take that two-week European vacation or early retirement yet, but you'll start to feel in control, and with control will come a very welcome sense of calm. From there you'll see lots of small wins like your first month contributing extra toward debt or your first month with no regrettable online shopping. These results will put you at ease, give you hope for recovery from your financial situation, and prove the vision for your future is possible.

So, let's not only consider short- and long-term goals, but present relief. There are wins you want to experience right now, not in a few months after you've been diligently budgeting. As you accomplish each goal, there's no win greater than the relief you feel as the pain of your money troubles lessens. It's like taking your hand off that hot stove! Removing your hand won't heal the wound, but it will stop it from getting worse.

FOCUS ON OVERCOMING YOUR PAST

Before you begin to move away from your present pain, I want you to think about how you got there. Yeah, I know what you're thinking, "Justin, do you want me to feel worse?" No, not at all. But I do want you to deal with and accept your past financial mistakes and move on. Do you know how long I held onto feelings of shame for my student loans, credit card debt, and absurd home purchase? At the time, all I could think about was how much money we'd have if I had gotten it together sooner.

If you had told me back then that all my biggest money blunders would be laid out in the introduction of a book, I think I'd have rolled over and died right there with my notebook, pen, and calculator still in hand. There's no reason to sit in your old mistakes. Isaiah 43:18 says, "Do not remember the past events, pay no attention to things of old." To move on and be successful, we've got to let go of the shame from past blunders that drag us down. Don't expect overnight change because the impact of these mistakes might not hit until you peel back the layers of your financial situation, but once you commit and start to see results, it'll get easier every day to forgive yourself. Don't forget this as you go through each level of the Pyramid. Even if you still feel regret at this point in the journey, forgive yourself, and forget what is behind.

SEEK CHECKPOINTS

As I mentioned, the elimination of your stress and pain doesn't all come at the end of the journey. Many of us dread the journey because we think there is nothing but pain all the way through. (Remember, even Sam and Frodo had some good times on the way to Mordor.) When we have the mindset of "it's all bad until the end," our hope for the future turns back to despair really fast, especially when we see a path that'll take years to complete. I remember feeling this way and thinking, *Maybe my pain isn't so bad? I can probably push money back and forth for the rest of my life and be content.* I can't tell you how glad I am that I didn't keep that defeatist outlook, because once I got started with the Financial Freedom Pyramid, I quickly hit small goals that felt huge to me. It was so encouraging, and it made every step of the journey easier having all these wins to document.

As you commit to the plan, don't fix your eyes only on the end. Keep it in the back of your mind, but don't focus on it too much when doing day-to-day money management. Instead, seek checkpoints. Checkpoints are places where you break down a larger goal into smaller bite-size chunks. Instead of expecting to scale the whole mountain at once, go a little ways and reach the first lookout. Work as hard as you can to have your first full month on a budget without overdraft fees or eating out or impulse shopping or whatever goal makes sense to you. Relish in all the relief and joy that comes from hitting that goal. Soon enough, you'll have $1,000 in the bank (won't that be great for your stress level?) and you'll pay off your first debt. These little checkpoint wins will start in the first few months or even weeks and keep coming. Finally, you'll believe in a bright future.

I know I'm getting a little ahead of myself because I haven't even told you what the plan is. But it's important to not forget there's a near future that frees you from so much of the hurt and struggle you experience every day. Financial freedom is just around the corner—always hold close the reasons why you want it so badly.

DON'T IGNORE YOUR GOALS

Once you form your goals, it's important you don't ignore them. Our human nature will do everything possible to rationalize our situation, break our habits, and cause us to forget about the objectives we've set for ourselves. Even when you really want something, it's hard to stay committed to the changes in behavior you have to make. You'll slip again and again unless you set up systems that keep you focused and remind you constantly of your short- and long-term goals.

Try to incorporate your goals into everything you do. If you wake up in the morning and pray, pray about your money. As you're getting ready for work, look at sticky notes on your bathroom mirror of your upcoming checkpoints.

When you drive to work, listen to personal finance podcasts and hear from other people like you striving for freedom with their money. When you're at work, tally up your hours and overtime to calculate the extra income you'll have for debt payoff. On the way home, remind yourself of your goals and make a plan for the evening that doesn't involve spending money. As you arrive at your house, practice gratitude, and note all the things you're happy with in your life. A spirit of contentment won't entice you to spend more money. At bedtime, recount all your financial wins for that day. I don't mean you should literally be thinking about money all day, but picking two or three of these exercises to do regularly is the most effective way to keep yourself aligned with your goals.

A TASTE OF FINANCIAL FREEDOM

Everyone's journey to financial freedom will look different—there's no one-size-fits-all—but the feeling of relief is the same, the release of pressure and the feeling of hope that leads to peace. What you've discovered throughout this chapter is what financial freedom can taste like beginning at the Awareness Level. You won't get true financial freedom until you reach the top of the Pyramid, but here on Level One, you start getting a sense of what that peace feels like. Some may get that taste of freedom after a month of no overdraft fees and extra cash to fix the broken kitchen sink. For others, they may not feel it until their emergency fund is bulked up (more on that in Chapter 4). Everyone gets a taste, though, and for everyone, the framework and the steps leading to true freedom are the same. To get there, you need to begin with the end goals in mind and know your why behind each of them, so you'll stay motivated throughout every level of the Pyramid.

Here's another example of a strong why making a big difference. I once had a single-dad client named Austin who came in flat broke with no idea how to get out of debt, let alone achieve financial freedom. He was a hard worker but couldn't seem to get ahead. Thankfully, his employer was gracious enough to pay for him to go through my coaching program because they felt so strongly about helping this determined man get ahead. Austin's big *why*? His three teenage daughters.

Like most parents, Austin wanted nothing but the best for his daughters. However, in his current financial state, he felt like if he didn't make some changes fast, his daughters' future would be on the line. Not literally, of course, but he thought their lack of opportunity due to his financial situation would impede their success. So, Austin's why was really clear: He wanted to secure a better life for his daughters despite his past financial mistakes.

One of the things I do during my coaching sessions is help identify victories and successes my clients accomplished since their last meeting. During Austin's first follow-up session, I asked him how creating and following his first budget went. I wasn't prepared for his profound response. He said, "This victory may not be a big deal to you, but it's a big deal to me. For over a decade, I have never once had any money left out of my paycheck by the time the next paycheck rolled around. However, last month, I still had twenty dollars in my pocket before the next paycheck. You have no idea how much that means to me. Seeing that twenty-dollar bill gave me hope that I *will* be able to reach my goals."

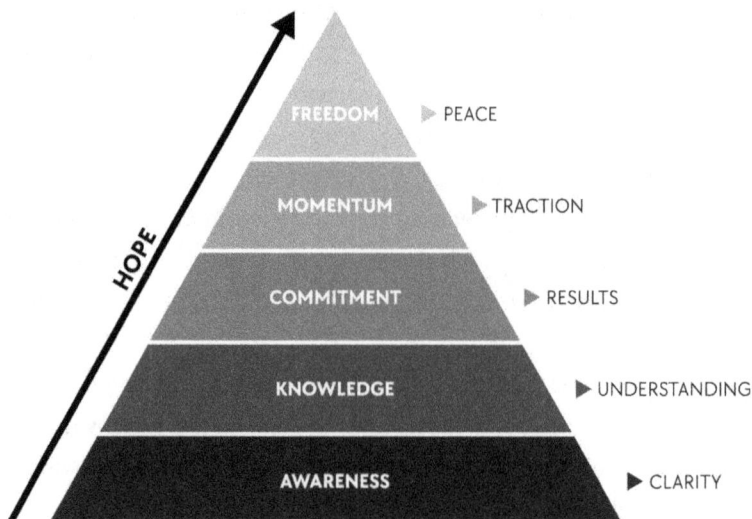

It gives me goosebumps every time I relive this session. Austin got a taste of freedom! It's these little things that make all the difference in the beginning. In fact, he shared new wins like this every session, and his employer got to see the weight slowly lift off his shoulders as he found hope in the process with every extra twenty-dollar bill. Austin had an understanding of his current pain and a firm grasp on the freedom that was waiting for him and his daughters. That made all the difference.

Here lies the divergence between despair and hope. When you realize where you are, you're full of despair. But that despair turns to hope for the first time in probably years when you have a clear and definite picture of where you're going. If you haven't already done so:

1. Review what you're currently spending and track all your expenses.
2. Write down your short- and long-term goals with your why for each one.
3. Write down on a separate piece of paper any past regrets or areas of shame you have associated with your finances. Begin the process of forgiving yourself so you can be free from the past and work toward financial freedom.

As you continue to take action, you'll begin to see progress that points to a hope-filled financial future forming in the distance. Let's waste no time jumping onto the next level of the Pyramid. It's time to establish some smart money practices, and with these tools, go from paycheck to paycheck to paycheck to freedom!

Chapter 2 Takeaways

- **Set short- and long-term goals.** Be sure your goals are *your* goals and that they're meaningful. Your goals also need to be in writing. You are much more likely to take your goals seriously if you write them down.

- **Have a strong why.** Having a strong why will help you avoid the Cycle of Regret when you're tempted to make a decision that will set you backwards on your financial journey.

- **Forgive yourself from past money mistakes.** No one is perfect. Everyone has made money mistakes. Learn from them, but more importantly, learn to forgive yourself. Life is too short to be held captive.

- **Seek checkpoints.** Breaking goals down into smaller goals will help you stay focused and keep you motivated all the way through the Pyramid.

- **Keep your goals top of mind.** Find at least two or three ways to keep your financial goals at the forefront of your mind. Put your goals where you can see them daily.

LEVEL TWO

Knowledge

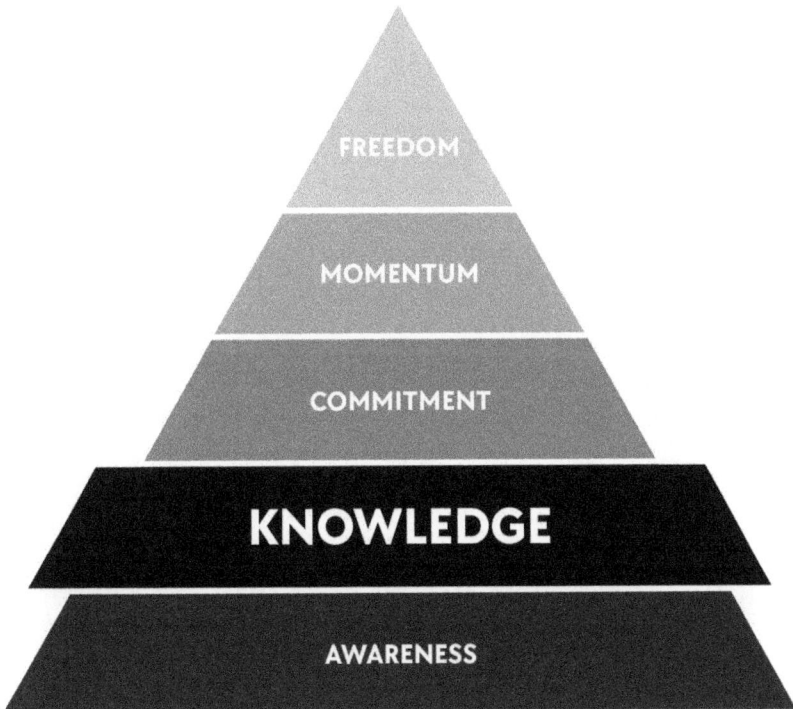

CHAPTER 3

Seven Proven Biblical Principles
for Finance

A steward's primary goal is to be found faithful.

—*Randy Alcorn,*
Managing God's Money

DID YOU KNOW MANY of the foundational money values necessary for the Knowledge Level of the Pyramid come from the Bible? Now, if you're not a Christian, you might be ready to dismiss this chapter's credibility right now. However, I encourage you to hang on for just a moment. These aren't principles that only traditional Christians follow. In fact, the concepts expressed in the 2,350 verses on money in the Bible are backed by research that affirm they are true and helpful for everyone. You probably already believe in, if not follow, some of the basics. Like a lot of great advice and wisdom, you may not have known it originally came from the Bible.

Maybe you're still reluctant—I get that! This is not the first time I've been met with skepticism because of my Christian values. I remember years ago, I phoned a young couple who were potential clients looking to get out of debt. I got a hold of the wife, and it was clear from the way she answered that she wasn't expecting a financial coach who was also a Christian. She snapped at me right away, saying, "Are you one of those God people?" I grinned and answered politely that yes I was. She replied, "We may want to work with you, but no God stuff." I agreed, no God stuff.

We moved forward despite obvious spiritual differences. When we got to the second session where I typically explain the Knowledge Level and teach my clients how money really works, I asked the wife, "I know I said no God stuff, and I am a man of my word, but would it be at all possible to share ten minutes of God stuff when it comes to finances?" She folded her arms and said, "You have ten minutes," and leaned back in her office chair ready to dismiss me outright.

I knew I didn't have much time, so I quickly explained these seven biblical principles of finance. I wanted to make sure we'd be on the same page and speaking the same language through the rest of the Pyramid. The whole point of the Knowledge Level is to set a solid, logical foundation where we can build the rest of our financial strategy. At the end of the session, I did what I always do and asked the couple about their "aha" moments and key takeaways from our conversation. The wife threw up her hands and said with surprise, "I can't believe I'm saying this, but my key takeaway was the freakin' God stuff." We both broke out in laughter because she did not use the PG word "freakin'," and the whole thing felt authentic, ironic, and refreshingly productive.

Though interactions like this for me are uncommon, people have a tendency to be a little wary of biblical concepts. It's normal and healthy for people to be skeptical about things when religion is involved. However, the principles you're going to read about aren't just biblical, they're actually common practices among wealthy people, religious or not, and they're backed by plenty of data. I've used these concepts as the foundation of my financial coaching business and seen thousands of families get on board with these principles, making unbelievable strides in their journey to financial freedom. So, in order to conquer the Knowledge Level, we've got to lay the groundwork with these seven proven biblical principles.[1]

PRINCIPLE ONE: ACKNOWLEDGE GOD'S OWNERSHIP (PSALM 24:1; PSALM 50:10)

How we perceive our money is a big factor that contributes to financial success or ruin. Have you ever been tempted to buy something you knew you shouldn't, and then told yourself, "I *should* buy this. I worked hard for this, and I really deserve it!" If your money was genuinely yours, this would check out. However, this never really works for you, does it?

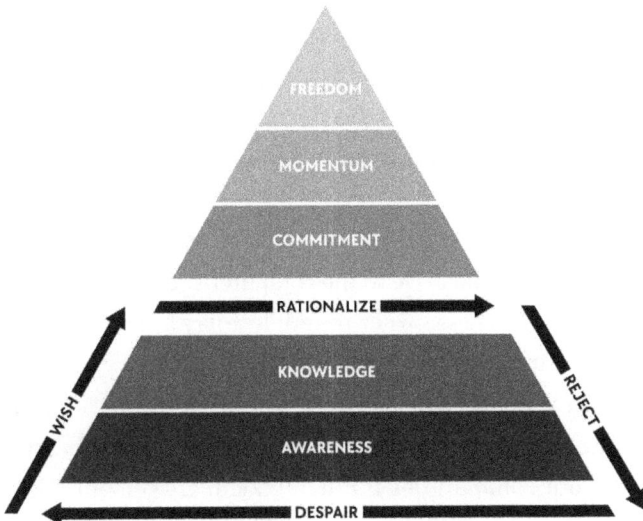

CYCLE OF REGRET

You end up overspending again and again because your job is stressful, your kids are wild, your days are busy, the weather is bad, or any other excuse to make yourself think you deserve a treat. All these potentially negative stimuli tell your brain, "Spend as much as you want." And you do. Before you know it, you're cracking open the pages of a personal finance guide, frustrated, scared, and overwhelmed.

The back and forth of "what I deserve" is a constant cycle that will never satisfy you. This goes for money and everything else. You may feel you deserve more alone time because your job is more intensive than your spouse's, or feel you deserve an extra-long vacation because of your recent promotion, despite your debt. Do these things ever lead to personal success? No. You end up feeling guilty, isolated, or underappreciated. This is the Cycle of Regret where you jump on board and rationalize a purchase or two, which leads to buyer's remorse and deep despair. This attitude of "I deserve whatever I want," doesn't work. Instead of thinking about your relationships, possessions, and money as yours and something you should have sole control over, think of it all as God's. Instead of asking ourselves what we want to do with our money, we should ask God, "What should I do with the money you've blessed me to manage?"

The Bible says in Luke 16:9–11 that the Lord has entrusted us with the money we have. He expects us to use the money He has given us wisely as a way of honoring Him. And if you're not a Christian, think of it as an exercise in thankfulness. There are a lot of people from all over the world that contribute to your well-being from the paved sidewalk you stroll on and the innovative car you drive to the computer software that makes your job easier and the business owner that didn't pay himself for months or even years to ensure you got a paycheck.

From a biblical perspective, passages like 1 Timothy 6:17–19 and Psalm 24:1 highlight God's will for us to use our money to better the lives of ourselves and our communities through good management. That means putting the money where God wants it, which is not always the same as where we want it. God says save? We spend fifty thousand on a camper. God says give? We hoard our money just in case the world ends. Newsflash: The world will end, and your rolls of hundreds aren't going to help much.

Study[2] after study[3] has shown that generous people benefit financially from their selflessness—in fact, they don't just make more money, they're also happier and reach their goals more often. Their reputation and the relationships they cultivate foster career growth and personal success. Society says, "Do whatever it takes to get to the top," but research tells us that we need to have a sacrificial and generous mindset to get to the top.

The point is when we remember we are simply stewards of our money, and that money needs to be used for a grander plan, we become less selfish and indulgent, and more careful and generous. With this comes financial prosperity and harmony. Every decision becomes logically and emotionally easier when you have an accurate perspective: It's not yours, it's God's!

PRINCIPLE TWO: SAVE MONEY (GENESIS 41:35–36; PROVERBS 21:20)

Yes, saving money is a biblical principle that leads to financial success. It may sound like a no-brainer, but saving money for future purchases really is counterculture. As a child, you may have saved up for the latest video game console or name-brand clothing item your parents weren't willing to spend that much money on, but since then, how often have you truly saved for big purchases?

If you're like many Americans, you put all big purchases on credit. You might have a car loan, student debt, various store credit cards, a regular credit card, and let's not talk about buy-now-pay-later services! It's actually no longer normal to save. We get what we want now and pay a little interest later, or at least that's how we perceive it. This might be hard to comprehend because we rarely do it anymore, but saving money is the most tried-and-true financial principle out there. In fact, every one of us has seen the fruit of savings at some point in our lives, even if it was when we were ten buying a new bike. (I can still remember flipping on my boombox for the first time after saving up for it for months!)

The Bible says, "Precious treasure and oil are in the dwelling of a wise person, but a foolish man consumes them" (Proverbs 21:20). Oh, we've all been there! Most of us have sat with our heads in our hands, trying to figure out how to pay for the car repair, the medical bill, or the kids' long list of school supplies because there's simply not enough. We find ourselves winding back the clock, regretting every foolish purchase we made in the past that led to our current situation. This is the despair state of the Cycle of Regret on overdrive!

You can't be certain of what unexpected expense will come up, that's why it's good to save and be prepared. Imagine the next time your car needs a repair and without having to stress, crunch numbers, and ask for help, you pull some cash from savings and take care of it. Any time life comes your way, your savings can create a buffer between you and financial chaos—and prevent you from surrendering to debt. Wow, doesn't that sound incredible?

Of course, I don't need to tell you that statistics tell us that saving more means a better financial picture and less stress. Whether you're saving for unexpected expenses, annual payments, or long-term financial goals, having the money piled up and ready will keep you at peace and will allow your income to do the most for you and your family.

PRINCIPLE THREE: LIVE ON LESS THAN YOU MAKE (1 TIMOTHY 6:6; HEBREWS 13:5)

The mindset of the world's wealthiest people might surprise you. Among what we've already discussed, research finds a core trait of almost every millionaire is frugality.[4] They preach living on less than they make to generate more savings, grow investments, give a higher percentage to charity, and overall win with money. Most don't advocate for buying large houses, brand new cars, and other big toys you can't afford. They tell you to spend less and make wise choices.

Of course, this state of discipline and contentment has its foundations in the Bible. I will never forget one of the first millionaires I met. It was a couple who had retired early by following these seven principles I'm discussing now. We were both at the same business meeting and after it ended, the man asked me if I wanted to know how he and his wife came to be millionaires. Becoming a millionaire can seem unreachable. Obviously, I wanted the secret sauce that would get my family and clients to that level of success. He leaned in and whispered in my ear as though he were guarding an industry secret that could get him offed by the likes of Tony Soprano and said, "Live on less than you make."

The couple was content with what God had given them and never convinced themselves they needed more than what they could pay for with cash, even long before they were millionaires. I've met more millionaires over the years, and this was the principle they said was foundational for their long-term success.

Our culture is bad at being content and living on less than they make. If we were good at it, we'd see far fewer Teslas, designer handbags, and trendy overpriced travel cups when we walked down the street. Of course, some people did save up to afford these luxuries, but the unfortunate truth is many did not. They're still making payments on the latest iPhone and the burger they ordered on UberEats a month ago. It's gotten completely out of control. We think these additional purchases will fill some void, but they always have us feeling guilty, insecure, and totally stressed out. That is why what the Bible says in 1 Timothy 6:6 is so true: "Godliness with contentment is great gain."

PRINCIPLE FOUR: PAY OFF DEBT (PROVERBS 6:1–11; PROVERBS 22:7)

In this section, I won't break down what your life should look like after debt. You have that image in your head already, I hope. If not, definitely take time to imagine your life without payments to any creditors at all. What does it look like? Sound like? Feel like? Take yourself back to Chapter 2 if need be and envision those short- and long-term goals.

Simply put, biblical principle number four says that debt should not be a normal part of anyone's life. The Bible says in Proverbs 22:7, "The rich rule over the poor, and the borrower is a slave to the lender." I once had an atheist tell me he could at least get behind that verse. (Hey, one verse out of the 31,102 verses in the Bible down. Only 31,101 to go!) It makes sense why he was open to this verse because doesn't it feel like you're a slave to the creditors you're shelling out tons of your hard-earned money to every month? Your credit purchases go well beyond your original bill with tons of added interest and fees, right? That's why God says to stay away from debt. A life of debt is one of unrest, shame, and bondage. You don't need the credit card. You don't need to take out student loans. You don't need a car payment. Debatably, none of it is ordained by

God according to His will in the Bible. The culture's glorification of debt isn't helpful, but completely harmful.

The average American household has over $104,000 of debt, which includes credit cards, retail cards, personal loans, car loans, student loans, and home equity lines of credit. That's not even including 401(k) loans, loans from friends and family, or outstanding medical bills. You read that right. The average household has over $104,000 of debt, not counting the mortgage![5] This is one of the reasons why 90 percent of adults are stressed about money, and it's why so many have no savings, no retirement, and no prospects of future growth.[6] It's all because of that debt tying them down. In order to become like one of those millionaires we've mentioned (or just become someone content with their wealth), you must take debt off the table. Dr. Thomas Stanley says in his book The Millionaire Mind:[7]

Early in my career of studying wealthy people, I had a glimpse of this segment of the millionaire population.... What I learned from them was simple, yet the message had a lasting impact on me. You cannot enjoy life if you are addicted to consumption and the use of credit.... All were first-generation wealthy. Some were credit dependent earlier in their careers, but they eventually saw the light. They went cold turkey, breaking the cycle of borrowing to consume, earning to consume, and borrowing more and more money. Others never became addicted to credit or the need to display their success.

Let me reiterate, debt can't be on the table. You've got to make the choice to never surrender to debt again. It doesn't matter if there is a sudden car repair or Christmas is coming fast. You're not going into debt. If you feel like you have been backed into a corner and can't see how to handle a given situation without borrowing, reach out to an accountability partner or financial coach and brainstorm other options.

I had a client cut up all his credit cards but one. He called me one day after one of his work trucks broke down and said, "Hey, I'm glad I kept that credit card. My truck broke down and it's going to cost $2,200 and I don't have the money to fix it." Now, I'm no mechanic, but after he shared what was wrong with his truck, I advised him to get two more quotes as something didn't sound quite right. He took my advice and got a quote for $850. He had $1,000 in savings, so he didn't need his credit card after all. Sometimes when things get stressful and overwhelming, you need that other voice to keep you on the straight and narrow.

I have never found a single person that was able to get out of debt and stay out of debt without having this mindset. Life will happen and in a weak moment you will swipe your credit card, get a bigger car loan, or justify borrowing on your house using a home equity loan or line of credit. As intense as it may sound, you have to look at debt as an enemy in the war waged for your financial freedom. Your vision for a prosperous and peaceful financial future can't include the continuation of credit card balances and loose principles.

PRINCIPLE FIVE: FOLLOW A WRITTEN PLAN (PROVERBS 21:5; LUKE 14:28–30)

"The plans of the diligent lead surely to abundance, but everyone who is hasty comes only to poverty" (Proverbs 21:5 ESV). Running through life without a plan will always result in ruin. No one accidentally gets anything. Instead, God's divine plan combined with your diligent planning leads you to your greatest potential. In order to win with money, you need a monthly budget. Each dollar that comes in and goes out needs to be planned. As you follow your budget from month to month, you'll get closer to your objectives rather than waiting for them to suddenly appear.

Luke 14:28–30 says,

For which of you, wanting to build a tower, doesn't first sit down and calculate the cost to see if he has enough to complete it? Otherwise, after he has laid the foundation and cannot finish it, all the onlookers will begin to make fun of him, saying, "This man started to build and wasn't able to finish."

Although this verse is teaching us to count the cost of salvation, the practical wisdom behind it is still true. Each month you have a mental picture on how you want the next thirty days to go. However, without a plan, every month you're running out of cash before the first of the next month comes around again. Then come the tears, the overdraft fees, the credit card swipes, the marital strain, and so much more. Poor planning with your money prevents you from seeing God's best, and it prevents you from executing God's best. There is no hope for savings, generosity, or investment when there's nothing left at the end of the month. In fact, there's often not enough to keep the lights on and gas in the car. It's a harsh reality, but it's true.

PRINCIPLE SIX: MAINTAIN YOUR FOUR WALLS (PROVERBS 18:10; 1 TIMOTHY 5:8)

The classic airplane safety adage, "Secure your mask before assisting others with theirs" is true. In an environment where oxygen is depleting, if you take time to help everyone else with their masks before you put on your own, you'll be out of air before you reach the third person. However, if you put your mask on first and get a steady stream of oxygen, you can help everyone around you.

The Bible, to many people's surprise, says the same about our finances. First Timothy 5:8 says, "But if anyone does not provide for his own, that is his own household, he has denied the faith and is worse than an unbeliever." Wow! Those are some strong words. But some Christians have warped senses of generosity where they give and give even when their own mouth isn't fed and there's no roof over their head. This may sound like "true generosity," but it's not. At my first job of my banking career, I was a mortgage collector who helped people get current on their homes, get them from being behind on their payments to being up to date on them before they hit foreclosure. It was not uncommon for me to see believers give to missionaries and other charities but were months behind on their mortgage and about to lose their homes. Not only can you not reach personal wealth if you don't take care of your four walls, but you also can't be as generous as you want. You're actually limiting your giving potential by focusing on generosity before taking care of your home and family.

If you're overwhelmed by the thoughts of paying off debt and building a savings because your lights are about to get shut off, please take care of your house before you give another dollar to a friend, charity, or ministry. Don't think about additional giving until you have your four walls sturdy. After that, you can save, give, and budget big time to meet your financial goals.

PRINCIPLE SEVEN: GIVE GENEROUSLY (MALACHI 3:10; 2 CORINTHIANS 9:7)

No matter your income level, you already know that giving is good. The question becomes "How much should I give?" Now, I'm not a theologian, a pastor, or an authority on God's will. You could take ten church leaders and you'd get ten different answers to this question. However, the Bible seems to express that your starting point with giving to the local church is 10 percent of your income—this is called a tithe. And 80 percent of my clients are able to tithe while getting out of debt even when they thought it would be totally impossible! When giving is done first and not last, it happens, and it works. God simply provides. Additionally, it puts our hearts in the right posture, remembering that we're only stewards of the money God has given us. This shift in our mindset adds another layer of accountability and makes discipline come easier compared to those who view their money as "what they deserve," which leads them to a lot of selfish and frivolous spending.

Often, even if you feel like you can't afford it, when you make giving a priority and figure out a way, you'll see tremendous changes in all aspects of your financial and spiritual life. Malachi 3:10 says, "Bring the full tenth into the storehouse so that there may be food in My house. Test Me in this way," says the Lord of Hosts. "See if I will not open the floodgates of heaven and pour out a blessing for you without measure." You heard it. Give, and be blessed. Remember, it isn't so much a rule as it is about your heart.

Not only does the Bible express the importance of giving in personal finance, a study by the Greater Good Science Center found that people who were more generous lived longer, were more active, had less stress, and were in overall better mental and physical health.[8] Additionally, the University of British Columbia found that generous people were happier and experienced more joy.[9] Another study published in the Journal of Personality and Social Psychology corroborated the other two studies and added that generous individuals tend to make more money and have more prosperous careers.[10] The point is God and secular research are in agreement: It pays to be generous!

This doesn't mean all your dreams will come true if you give, but it does mean that as you submit to the Lord with your finances, the path ahead will become clearer, and you'll be able to take the next steps up the Pyramid with wisdom, peace, and joy.

PROSPERITY STARTS WITH A PLAN

These seven biblical principles are the foundation to a healthy and prosperous financial future. Both the Bible and independent research have confirmed that when you follow these standards for personal finance, you'll find hope and success ahead. Take time to consider each of these principles and determine how you will make them your own. If you want a deeper dive into biblical principles and finances, I highly recommend Randy Alcorn's book *Managing God's Money*.[11]

Chapter 3 Takeaways

- **There are 2,350 verses on money in the Bible, and their truths are backed by research.** The Knowledge Level sets a solid, logical foundation where you can build the rest of your financial strategy.

- **Contentment is foundational for long-term success.** Learning how to save and live on less than you make is vital to achieve financial freedom.

- **Never surrender to debt again.** If you are okay with borrowing money, even for emergencies, you won't obtain debt freedom.

- **Live by a written plan called a budget.** Planning ahead for how you are going to use your income will help you win with your money. Remember to pay your necessities first which are food, shelter, utilities, transportation, and clothing.

- **It pays to be generous.** When giving is done first and not last, it puts our hearts in the right posture, remembering that we're only stewards of the money God has given us. Multiple studies have found that people who were more generous lived longer, were more active, had less stress, and experienced more joy.

CHAPTER 4

Focused Steps for a Strong Foundation

Success demands singleness of purpose. You need to be doing fewer things for more effect instead of doing more things with side effects.

—*Gary Keller,*
The One Thing

DID YOU EVER PLAY the game *Whac-A-Mole*? For those of you that need your memory jogged, or for those of you too young to step foot in a 1980s arcade, *Whac-A-Mole* was a game where you'd hold a mallet while little rubber moles popped up out of various holes on a game cabinet. You'd be tasked with "whacking" the mole with the mallet before it quickly slipped back under the surface.

The game starts slow, and you can easily hit each mole and watch your score rise on the scoreboard. Soon enough, though, the moles pop up and drop down faster and faster—multiples at a time. At that point, it's impossible to hit all the moles. You start to get frustrated and frantic, and that score doesn't rise nearly as quickly as it did in the beginning. In fact, by the end of the game, you usually feel more like a loser than a winner. When you finished playing *Whac-A-Mole*, your body was tired, your mind was agitated, and you knew you missed a lot of opportunities. Why? Because you were doing way too much at once! We often try to do everything at the same time with our money too, as though we're playing a lifelong game of *Whac-A-Mole*, except we don't want our money management to be needlessly difficult like an arcade game.

Just like with the game, your money has you tired, agitated, and missing opportunities for success. How many things are you working on right now? There's a good possibility you're already juggling a lot, trying to solve all your money problems at the same time. Like many clients before they work with me, you may be trying to

- Pay off debt
- Build an emergency fund
- Invest in the stock market
- Save for a house
- Save for children's college
- Save for a big purchase like a car
- Invest in retirement
- Invest in real estate
- Pay off the house
- Start a business
- Save for a family vacation
- Give generously

None of the objectives above are bad at all. In fact, I want you to accomplish all these goals. However, trying to do all these at once will get you nowhere. You'll get overwhelmed by the lack of progress and one day you'll be surprised by how little the needle has moved in certain categories. Sure, maybe you are finally contributing to your 401(k), but you haven't paid off your debts that'll follow you well into retirement. Or maybe you're saving for the kids' college education, but you have no flexible money in your savings account. Remember, a win and a loss in finances is still a loss.

The order you do things in your financial plan is important, and I would argue that doing one thing at a time is just as important. When you can focus on one goal at a time, you can make fast, measurable progress that keeps you moving. Momentum will build as you get encouragement and motivation from your wins, no matter how small they are in the beginning.

So, what's the outline for the ideal plan that'll get you to financial freedom? I use Dave Ramsey's "Baby Steps," a seven-step process to achieve all your money goals. We will be focusing on the first three Baby Steps, (1) save $1,000 for your starter emergency fund, (2) pay off all consumer debt using the debt snowball method, and (3) save three to six months of living expenses in a fully-funded emergency fund. The Baby Steps are the best way to help you live out the seven biblical principles from Chapter 3.

No matter who you are and what you want to accomplish with your money, these Baby Steps will get you there. They're universal, they're simple, and they're fool-proof. If you've been searching for a plan or system to fix your financial situation, you've probably already come across the Baby Steps or may have even tried them. If that's you, don't give up yet. The Baby Steps are still the answer to reaching your goals—some people just need a few more tools to make the steps work for them.

BABY STEP 1: $1,000 (STARTER) EMERGENCY FUND

If you've ever tried attacking your debt and investing in the future, what always gets in the way? Let me guess: unexpected repairs, unexpected income loss, unexpected medical expenses, unexpected veterinary bills, unexpected doomsday bunker construction costs—okay, maybe not that last one. The point is unexpected stuff is always headed our way. When we try to pay off debt, make big purchases, and invest when there's no emergency fund, we're constantly getting behind, even if we're following a budget and a set plan. If we can prepare for these unexpected occurrences, we can accomplish way more with our money. We just need a little wiggle room.

So, for Baby Step 1, you need to save $1,000 for your starter emergency fund which should take one to two months to complete. Now, it's true this won't cover huge repairs or a job loss, but it's enough money to keep you from spiraling back to financial disaster. Most potential emergencies won't require a thousand dollars up front; however, if yours does, you will have some time to figure out how you're going to make up the rest without derailing all your financial plans. You may have to sell some things from around the house, rideshare, sell plasma (but keep all your organs, there are better ways to get cash), get an extra job, start a side business, or rent out a room, but you can get there. Take a moment to consider how you will get to your $1,000 goal.

This is important: Your emergency fund should be in a separate bank account used exclusively for emergencies. It's not a vacation fund or an I'm-too-tired-to-cook-so-let's-go-out-to-eat fund or a cushion for your checking account in case you're hit with an overdraft fee. It's meant to be saved and not accessed unless absolutely necessary. The reason you keep it in a separate account is mainly psychological. It's like having a pull-down fire alarm behind a glass casing. It's there in case of an emergency, but you have to break the glass to use it. The extra step, by design, should make you hesitate.

Baby Step 1 is important for not only getting over some financial hurdles but getting over emotional ones too. Like 69 percent of Americans,[1] my wife, Jessica, and I didn't have $1,000 in our savings account. (Even more shocking, 34 percent of Americans don't even have one dollar saved.[2]) We used our overdraft protection as our emergency fund. Each month we'd pay a little off, and max it out again. Then, we'd pay it off, max it out, and do it all over again. We were on edge all the time and frantically checking our accounts every day. You may do this with a credit card or a buy now, pay later service. Whatever it is, it's debt, not an emergency fund, and it doesn't actually save you anything.

When my wife and I finally saved up our $1,000 emergency fund, it was the first time we felt any kind of relief from the anxiety we carried. Don't get me wrong, we were still stressed. We had over $100,000 in debt to pay off! However, before the emergency fund, we felt like we couldn't breathe, like we were expected to run a race while wearing a mask. We had this long road ahead of us to pay off all this debt and change our money habits, but we couldn't do it because we could not catch our breath. With that $1,000 in savings, though, we got a little air and a little hope we could reach financial freedom. We not only could run longer but faster toward our goals. Plus, it inspired us to find more ways to release pressure and race even quicker to financial freedom. This $1,000 emergency fund was the kick-starter for us. And our experience was not an anomaly. No matter who you are or how much debt you have, Baby Step 1 will give you that first oxygen burst of power over your finances. I know you may have some questions, so let's tackle a few of the most common ones.

"My income is very low. How do I save $1,000?"

If you make less than $20,000 a year, you only need to save $500 to complete Baby Step 1.

"My budget is tight. I don't know how I'm going to save up $1,000!"

This step is meant to be done quickly because, like I mentioned, $1,000 is not much money for all the emergencies that could come your way. However, I understand that saving that amount is easier for some households than for others. To save $1,000, don't just look at where you can cut your budget, also look at where you can add income.

Sure, cutting expenses is great, but if your budget is full of necessities you can't budge on, it's time to get to work. I'm not talking about your day job, I mean another job on the weekends, at nights, on holidays, or during the Superbowl or the season finale of *The Bachelor*. It sucks, I know. I did it too! But remember this is for a short period until you get that money. Buckle down, get to work, sell things, and cut expenses to get your $1,000.

I once met with a single mom named Crystal who had nothing saved for an emergency fund. Crystal knew she needed to have one, but couldn't see how it was possible, especially with very little wiggle room in her initial budget. We took a moment to brainstorm some ideas and decided her best approach to reaching her goal would be to sell some things around the house. Although she didn't think there'd be much to sell, to her surprise, the first week she found $200 worth of items that quickly sold online. These were little things like small appliances she didn't use, clothes the kids had grown out of, and a few like-new pairs of shoes she'd kept for special occasions. She felt nothing but relief as those items left her front step. Less clutter, more savings, a win-win.

That small win sparked in her a belief that she could find more things to sell around the house. She dug a little deeper, beyond the stuff that felt easy to get rid of. Each day, she'd do a lap around her house and challenge herself to find something to sell. Of course, that meant the sting of selling items got a little sharper every time she did a lap. First, went some non-essential home decor items, then the treadmill, then a set of nice dishware, and then the tablet. Yep. Two kids at home and she sold the tablet, but she was committed and knew they'd have plenty of ways to keep themselves entertained before they got another one. However, she hadn't quite reached her goal, so she sold a gold and diamond necklace that she'd been gifted years earlier. It was tough, but she decided she wanted her family's financial security more than the expensive accessory. By the end of the month, Crystal had her $1,000!

The point is the money is probably available to you in one way or another. Sometimes, you've just got to dig deep and figure it out. Crystal couldn't work more than two jobs and had to always consider where her children would stay while she was at work. Some of you may have similar constraints such as transportation limitations or health problems. Whatever it is, you can overcome it and find a way to make some extra cash. As you work to save up your emergency fund, push yourself a little more each day until you hit your goal. You'll get there in no time with the right mindset.

"I have more than $1,000 in savings. What do I do with that money?"

Are you ready for this? What I am about to tell you will either feel really good or really bad, but I promise you it's what's best. You need to put all that additional money toward debt—all of it aside from your $1,000 emergency fund. For example: If you have $10,000 in savings, I would tell you to put $9,000 of it towards your debt. The natural knee-jerk reaction would be, "Whoa, Justin. I can't do that. It's too risky." You're right. It is risky. But what's even more risky is ignoring your debt. By having you take the bulk of your savings to pay off debt, your emotions now run parallel with reality— that you're broke! In short, having too much money in your emergency fund while still owing debt is a false safety net that doesn't protect you from anything. A safety net when you're in debt is like stockpiling extinguishers while your house is on fire. By the time you finally feel like you have enough to put out the blaze, your house will already be burned to the ground. That's an extreme metaphor, but I think it really speaks to the frivolity of stacking up cash in the bank when you're making payments all over the place (with interest too).

Remember the sports car story? It's easier to move away from pain than toward pleasure—the low emergency fund will be that pain through the first few Baby Steps. So, keep only $1,000 in your emergency fund (or if that makes you too anxious, bump it up to $2,000, but no more), and start the momentum of your debt-free journey.

"What do I do if I have to use my emergency fund?"

You finally have $1,000 in savings. Yay! And then, bummer, something comes up like a car repair. Well, guess what? That's what the emergency fund is for. However, before you use your emergency fund, ask yourself if the "emergency" could actually wait a month or two. If that's the case, you could edit your budget (you will learn how in Chapter 6) to pay for the expense in cash instead of depleting your emergency fund. This is the better option.

However, if it is an emergency and you have no other funds to use or options to consider, then use your emergency fund. That is what it's there for. Don't hold onto guilt, feel ashamed, or defeated. This is totally normal, and is exactly how your emergency fund is meant to be used. After the emergency is over, quickly replenish your $1,000 emergency fund before going back to making extra payments toward debt in Baby Step 2.

BABY STEP 2: DEBT SNOWBALL

If you're like the average American, debt has been a normal part of your life up to this point. You took out student loans because that's what everyone did. You got a new car because the Internet told you it'd be more reliable. You got a big house, so it could be your "forever home." You financed everything from the new laptop you needed for school to the eight-dollar coffee you grabbed every morning. You put anything you couldn't afford at the time on a credit card, because you were 100 percent sure you were going to pay it off the next month. (Side note: Did you know only 35 percent of credit card holders actually pay off their credit cards every month?[3])

All this "normal thinking" has you drowning in a giant pile of debt. It's so huge now, it doesn't seem like you'll ever get on top of it. You might feel so defeated that you don't see a point in trying to fix it. In fact, why not pile on more? What's the harm at this point? Let me tell you, you can get ahead of this! I did it, so I know it's possible. You just need to focus on one thing at a time (remember *Whac-A-Mole*) and commit to the grind. It's going to take a lot of work and hours to dig yourself out, but once you do, your life will be new. Getting out of debt is one of the hardest things someone can do, but it's also one of the most rewarding.

To get started, first take your list of debts you wrote down from Chapter 1 and arrange them from smallest balance to largest balance. Don't consider the interest or the possibility of forgiveness or anything like that. Simply put them in order of balance. Once you have that, you can start your debt snowball. Here's how: Pay the minimum payments on every debt except your smallest one. Then, throw everything you have at that smallest debt. It'll feel a lot like Baby Step 1, where you work your butt off to get that $1,000 saved up and achieve that quick win. That's how you're going to feel when you get that first debt paid off.

After that first debt is gone, you'll take what you were paying on that debt, and roll it into the next one, while continuing to pay the minimum payments on the others. Each time you pay off a creditor, like a snowball, your contribution to the next debt increases, which means the debts go down faster after each debt is paid off. I'm telling you, it's so motivating to see the speed pick up as you're working through your debt. With this method, regardless of that starting total, most people get out of debt between one and three years.

Just think about it. In under three years you could be free from debt. Not just free from the stress and worry, but free from those crippling payments too. All those payments evaporate at the end of Baby Step 2, and all that cash will become available to you again. With all those debt payments gone, it'll feel like you got a raise, and for some of you, a substantial one! That $700 isn't going to the bank for the car loan. That $300 isn't going to the credit card company. That $250 isn't going to your student loan provider—it's going to you.

DEBT SNOWBALL

DEBT	BALANCE	MINIMUM PAYMENT	NEW PAYMENT
Medical Bill 1	$600	$50	*N/A
Medical Bill 2	$1,200	$100	$150
Visa	$6,000	$100	$250
Master Card	$7,000	$147	$397
Student Loan 1	$15,000	$134	$531
Student Loan 2	$20,000	$173	$704
Car Loan	$25,200	$690	$1,394
TOTAL	$75,000	$1,394	

*After the first debt is paid off, you would add the $50 payment in this example to the next debt in the snowball.

Once that money is back in your hands, you can really do some amazing things. Think about how much easier saving, investing, and giving will be with that kind of money released back to you. Moving toward your goal of financial freedom suddenly becomes much simpler, and you can get there much faster than you ever thought possible with a few extra hundreds or thousands in the bank every month. We'll talk more about this period of your journey on the Momentum Level of the Pyramid. Before we move on, let's tackle some more common questions you may have.

"I understand I'm supposed to pay off the smallest loan first, but shouldn't I pay in order of highest interest rate?"

If you love math and hard logic, you probably already crunched the numbers and realized you'd pay less to all the creditors if you paid off the highest interest loan first. But if you were concerned about how to mathematically save money, you wouldn't have taken out all these loans and credit cards in the first place, right?

What we're up against is not math. What we're up against is behavior. (And probably a little financial trauma!) You need to feel the power of the snowball effect, so you have the motivation and momentum to take down one debt after the other without giving up and falling into the Cycle of Regret. Paying off large loans first won't give you the energy and drive you need to tackle all the debt you have. Starting with the biggest debt will feel as discouraging as trying to pay them all down at once. Harvard did a study that proved paying off the smallest balance first is by far the most effective method of ditching debt.[4]

It makes sense. If you had a small hatchet and were trying to chop down an enormous oak tree, you'd put in a lot of effort and see very little results. You'd hack away at it, only making insignificant scratches in the trunk, and maybe you'd chip off some bark too. With lots of time and hard work, the tree would remain unshaken. Would you continue to use that tool to take down the tree? No way! That's what it's like to pay off those higher debts and higher interest rates first. Even though eventually that tree would come down, you're not creating any momentum. You won't have the traction needed to take this thing all the way to the end.

So don't look at the interest rates. Focus on one small debt at a time. When you finally get to the big debts, they won't seem that big when compared to the huge payment you'll be able to put toward them. You'll be cutting down that enormous tree with a high powered chainsaw instead of a small hatchet.

"Do I keep building my emergency fund during this time?"

The goal is to keep only $1,000 in your emergency fund until all your consumer debt is paid off. The reason is the more money you have in savings, the less urgency you will have in paying off your debts.

However, there is an exception to this rule. If a financial storm pops up, such as a job loss, an upcoming move, or a new baby, pause your debt snowball and build that savings as much as possible. Hopefully, this will help you weather the storm and get through without surrendering again to debt. Once you're on the other side of it, use any additional funds above $1,000 towards paying down your debt. Continue the debt snowball and pat yourself on the back for getting through the financial mess without swiping another credit card or taking out another loan. Even though you had to take a break from the debt snowball, this is still a big win!

Even if you're really driven to pay off your debt and you think you can get through the storm without stopping, I recommend pausing anyway until you know for sure. I worked with a couple named Tori and James a few years ago, and after a few sessions, Tori announced that she was pregnant. She and James were insistent that they could continue their debt snowball because they had fantastic health insurance. All their research told them that medical bills would not be an issue. I loved their motivation, but I encouraged Tori and James to put money away anyway, because you just never know what could happen.

They did what I recommended, and it was a good thing too. When Tori and her husband started working on the nursery, they found the room was riddled with mold under the carpet and in the walls. It wasn't cheap to fix, and absolutely had to be fixed before they brought their child into the world. Thankfully, Tori and James had an emergency fund to get the mold taken care of because their health insurance wouldn't cover it. So, if you see a storm coming, pause Baby Step 2 until it passes, then continue paying off your debt until you have none.

BABY STEP 3: THREE TO SIX MONTH EMERGENCY FUND

Here's where you really start to feel waves of freedom and hope. In fact, you might be feeling pretty good about yourself and your situation when you start Baby Step 3, but don't let off the gas. Keep powering through and working extra hard. In this step, you are converting your Baby Step 1 emergency fund to a Baby Step 3 emergency fund. You will use your "raise" from the debt payments you no longer have and turn your $1,000 emergency fund into a fully funded emergency fund of three to six months of living expenses. Keep in mind, this is three to six months of living expenses, not income, and most people complete this step in six to twelve months. Now, with your fully funded emergency fund, you'll really get a taste of financial freedom. Imagine it. No more stress when you have an unpaid sick day, the car needs to be repaired, or you have a sudden trip to the ER after your kid breaks a bone on the playing field. The Baby Step 3 emergency fund can cover it all, so you can keep focusing on the future.

If you're wondering whether you should save three, four, five, or six months of expenses, know that for the average person, I recommend three months. This is usually about $10,000–$30,000 in the bank. A household with $4,000 per month of living expenses would keep a minimum of $12,000 in their emergency fund. But if you have inconsistent income or need more in savings to manage anxiety from past financial trauma, go ahead and bump it up to six months.

If at any point your emergency fund drops below three to six months of living expenses, return to Baby Step 3 and get it back to the set number.

NO MORE GAMES

Instead of using a frantic, hit-and-miss approach to your finances, work smarter with a steady pace and the knowledge that the Baby Steps work. As you scale the Financial Freedom Pyramid and complete the three Baby Steps, you'll feel more peace than you've probably felt since childhood. You'll be free from both the stress of debt and the stress from upcoming expenses. You'll have peace and the ability to do so much more with your money. Not only will you be able to fix that broken window or replace that outdated phone, but you'll be able to grow the kind of wealth you've always wanted to, living life to the fullest, while being incredibly generous in the process.

Chapter 4 Takeaways

- **Focus on one thing at a time while building your financial foundation.** The order you do things in your financial plan is important. When you can focus on one goal at a time, you can make fast, measurable progress that keeps you moving.

- **Use the first three Ramsey Baby Steps to achieve financial freedom.** The steps are (1) save $1,000 for your starter emergency fund, (2) pay off all consumer debt using the debt snowball method, and (3) save three to six months of living expenses in a fully-funded emergency fund.

- **Save $1,000 for your starter emergency fund.** This essential step on your way to financial freedom should be completed within one to two months.

- **Use the debt snowball to pay off all consumer debt.** List your debts from smallest to largest by balance, paying the minimum payments on all debts but the smallest one. Apply every extra dollar you can find to the payments on the smallest debt. When the smallest debt is paid off, take what you were paying towards that debt and apply it to the next smallest-balance debt. Repeat this process until all your consumer debt is paid off within one to three years.

- **Build a fully funded emergency fund of three to six months of living expenses.** Use your "raise" from the debt payments you no longer have and turn your $1,000 emergency fund into a fully funded emergency fund that should take between six to twelve months to complete.

The True Identity of Your Budget

Look at our society. Everyone wants to be thin, but nobody wants to diet. Everyone wants to live long, but few will exercise. Everybody wants money, yet seldom will anyone budget or control their spending.

—John C. Maxwell,
1000+ John C. Maxwell Quotes

ONE OF MY OLDEST CLIENTS was an eighty-one-year-old woman named Betty. Betty had $12,000 of debt and was struggling to make ends meet. This incredible woman, who was smart, charismatic, and a great worker, was putting in sixty hours a week for nine dollars an hour. Yeah . . . you might want to go back and read that again. Sixty hours a week for nine dollars an hour. No, this was not 2004. And she had been working for over fifty years at steady, stable jobs. This woman had plenty of skills and solid references. If she was working sixty hours a week at age eighty-one, imagine how hard she worked at age twenty or thirty.

Betty and her husband had never been on a budget before, so when he died, she had to continue working. Even after all those years in the workforce,

Betty was still trying to get out of debt and reach her much-deserved retirement. That's when she reached out to me for some help. Of course, the first thing I did was get her on a budget. Each month we'd plug all the numbers into her budget spreadsheet and Betty would stick to it. Despite staying disciplined, after each monthly session, she would ask, "Justin, where did all my money go?"

I was confused every time. I'd kindly gesture to the spreadsheet with her budget typed on it and say, "Betty, it's all right here."

Unfortunately, each time I said it she wasn't satisfied. There was no burst of realization, no wash of cool relief, no wave of newfound confidence. She looked dismayed every session. This is not the way you want a client to look after they successfully complete and follow a budget. I wanted her to feel encouraged and empowered, but Betty made it clear with her hopeless stare that was not happening.

After the third session and her third round of asking me the same question, I finally responded differently. "Now Betty, you've asked me that question every time we've met. I feel like we must be talking about different things. Can you explain what you mean?" She gave a big sigh and looked right at me as she said with a strong but regretful voice, "Justin, my husband and I worked our butts off for over five decades, and I can honestly say I do not know where any of our hard-earned money went."

I was breathless. Can you imagine faithfully working day after day, sacrificing so much to make a good life for your family, and then at eighty-one years old, you have nothing to show for it? I will say Betty had plenty of wealth outside of money. She had a strong faith in God, a close family, a great personality, and an unbeatable Scrabble-winning streak, but as far as money and significant assets? Zilch. Nada. Nothing.

Before I could respond, she got a spark of ferocity in her eyes. She waved her finger at me in a way only a grandmother could and said, "You tell everyone younger than me to get on a budget *now*. I do not want anyone to be where I am in my eighties—widowed and with nothing to show for her years of work." She didn't waste time feeling sorry for herself. Instead, she stuck with me for a few years and got out of debt. But I'm sorry to say Betty is still working. It's too late for her to make the kind of necessary changes required to achieve a peaceful retirement. Her message to you, though, should ring loud in your ears and heart. Don't wait! Get on a budget now and set yourself up for future success. You'll find out as Betty did that getting on a budget actually gives you a sense of peace and control that you've been craving all your adult life.

It's not just Betty who had this regret, wishing she'd gotten on a budget sooner. Sixty-seven percent of households don't have a written financial plan![1] Almost every client I have echoes the same refrain, "I wish I'd done this sooner." So many future mistakes and mishaps can be avoided if we just make the change now. Committing to a budget won't be smooth at first, but eventually it will. The most important thing you can do in this whole process of getting a handle on your finances is to get on a budget and stick to it. Once you understand the philosophy and process of a budget, it becomes a lot easier. If you're sitting there still unsure about starting a budget, it's probably due to one of three reasons:

1. You don't think you need one because of your income or spending habits.
2. You don't want anything preventing you from enjoying your money.
3. You're afraid of what you'll find out.

Let's explore and challenge each one of these thoughts. Before I can coach you all the way to the Freedom Level, I need you on board with a budget. Your ticket out of your financial mess is making your own income work for you using this system.

"I don't need a budget."

This one is easy to debunk. There's this myth that when you make a lot of money or "enough" money, you don't need a budget. I'll tell you that's just plain wrong. Remember in Chapter 3, one of the common habits among millionaires, even with their millions, was to live on less than they made. If you're going to live on less than you make, you have to know how much you make and how much you spend. It's that simple. Millionaires have budgets because that's how they became millionaires and how they stay millionaires. Budgets aren't something you do when things are tight or when you're poor.

It's a way of planning and prioritizing where your hard-earned cash goes, so you get the most value from your money. Doesn't that sound great? A budget will give you the full fruits of your labor. No more looking at your bank account and feeling dejected, realizing your paycheck has been swallowed up despite your hours and hours of diligent work. Eighty-three percent of people that set financial goals feel better about their finances after just one year.[2] One year! The truth is a budget helps prioritize what is important to you, allowing you to more fully enjoy what is important to you and brings you to a place of contentment.

"I deserve to enjoy my money."

When we work hard, we often want to reward ourselves. Maybe a few months of working long hours prompts you to schedule a vacation. Maybe an early morning schedule means you buy expensive, made-to-order coffee. Maybe a stressful day warrants some retail therapy. Or maybe you have strict ultimatums on things you won't give up. On the surface, this isn't necessarily a bad thing. Budgeting is about prioritizing, not giving up everything that brings you joy. That's why I wasn't rattled when clients Kate and Aaron told me early on, "There are two things we will not cut out of our budget, and that's vacations and gym memberships."

Before making a comment, I consulted the budget form they filled out. To my surprise, their sacred gym memberships category was left blank. I asked them how much it cost each month, so I could help them decide if keeping it would help them reach the Freedom Level.

"$500 per person per month," Kate said.

"How many gym memberships are you paying for?"

"All of us."

I cocked my head and my eyes went wide. There were four people in this family. Kate, Aaron, and their two teenage boys. I had to ask again because I was certain I'd misheard. "So . . . all four of you have a $500 per month gym membership?"

"Absolutely," she said.

Making a great effort to not show the shock on my face, I calculated this out loud. "Okay, $500 times four memberships means you're paying $2,000 a month."

"Wait, what? Say that again?" Kate leaned in, brows raised.

"You're paying $24,000 a year for gym memberships."

"Really?" she said. I saw on her face a jolting awareness moment like I had years ago on that warm June day. Her husband looked similarly dumbfounded.

In fairness, this couple made over $24,000 a month after taxes, but this was still a crazy amount of money to spend for something non-essential. They were also paying almost $10,000 in debt payments each month, not including their house payment. That's almost $120,000 a year in debt payments alone.

Kate and Aaron were very uncomfortable and unhappy with these gym-membership numbers. After a few moments Kate scoffed and said, "Oh ... we're *definitely* finding another gym." And they did too. They reduced their monthly gym rates to $300 for all four people. However, prior to breaking down the numbers for them, Kate and Aaron were convinced that their family deserved this expensive gym membership. Once they heard what it was really costing them and how it was probably costing them their goal of financial freedom, they developed the right mindset and found a much less expensive alternative. If you're in debt and struggle living paycheck to paycheck, you don't "deserve" a $2,000 gym membership no matter how hard you work. Even if you're a top-rated customer satisfaction specialist at the DMV.

Hear me out. I want you to be rewarded for your work. Budgeting doesn't stop that. It just facilitates it in a more logical way, so you achieve bigger gains in the future. Think about it this way: If you're trying to lose weight, but every time you work out, you reward yourself with a bountiful dinner of cheeseburgers and hot fudge sundaes, you'd never reach your goal. Do you deserve a pat on the back for getting up at 5 a.m. to go to the gym? Do you deserve a celebration for fighting your food cravings? Yes! However, you don't want to reward yourself with something that actually punishes you by limiting your long-term gain.

Let's also not forget the mistakes that got you to this point. I am not here to play the blame game at all, in fact, I want you freed from past guilt. But I will push back a bit on clients when they feel entitled to live a lavish lifestyle they simply can't afford. Remember, you got yourself into this mess, which means "treating yourself" really shouldn't be on the table. What you really deserve is to get out of the mess. So, when you're mourning the loss of your morning coffee, your stress-relieving online shopping, or your $2,000 gym membership remind yourself that though you work hard, you've got to right some wrongs.

Before you start imagining Mark Cuban's mustard and ketchup sandwich diet,[3] relax. A budget will afford plenty of rewards—maybe not as extravagant or expensive as you're used to—but your rewards will never be "despite" your budget, they'll be intentional, planned, and affordable.

"I'm scared of what I'll find out."

This is a fear most of my clients have. Starting a budget is terrifying if you've never sat down to total up your expenses, calculate your monthly deficit, or add together your total debt. Up to this point, you've been able to keep this door shut. It's like when one of your kids is a slob and you know their room needs a biohazard unit to make it liveable, but you choose not to open the door in hopes someday it'll magically get better or your child will have a sudden burst of tidy inspiration.

Well, I have news for you. Your money will never clean itself up (and neither will your teenager, without help). The point is you've got to take a deep breath and look at the state of your finances, no matter how bad it might look. When you're feeling overwhelmed at the thought of looking this thing in the eyes, think about Betty. You've got time! You can right this wrong long before she did. Plus, you'd be surprised how many of my clients discover their situations aren't as bad as they thought. However severe the problem, you can get on a budget and have a prosperous and peaceful future, but first . . . we've got to assess the damage.

BUDGETS DON'T CONTROL YOU, THEY LIBERATE YOU

I'll admit, there are several challenges people face when getting on a budget. One of the biggest struggles is feeling controlled or confined by their budget. Most clients come in thinking their budget will feel like their dictator, telling them every day what they can and cannot do; however, that's not what a budget is, and that's never how it works. A budget is nothing more than a strategic shopping list. Clients tell me when they get intentional with their budget, they actually feel liberated and set free, not trapped or controlled.

Think about how money makes you feel now. Stressed, anxious, stupid, irresponsible, weak, and resentful. You constantly feel pushed to spend, but then you feel guilty for spending. When you try to save, the money gets jerked away from you anyway, somehow, somewhere. Most of the time, you don't feel like you get to do anything with your paycheck before it dissipates, getting distributed to creditors, banks, utility companies, and all the other stuff. You feel sucked dry, and to get out, you become dependent on the system that got you there, taking out loans and more credit cards.

This money in your pocket is like a bad relationship. It's gaslighting you, giving you a false sense of security, and tossing you back and forth between overindulgence and shame. That is control. That feels like a dictatorship. How you're living now, with no budget or set financial principles, is not freedom—it's cleverly disguised captivity. But you can break free with a good budget. With a budget, you don't have to feel guilty about spending anymore. No, seriously! Right now, when you swipe your debit card at the grocery store, you're praying it doesn't decline. If the transaction does go through, you're praying the amount leftover is enough for tomorrow's bills. Spending is chaotic for your brain whether you spend $50 or $500. You never know what you can afford and what you can't. It's as though you can't afford anything, as if you're shackled. When you have a budget, and that budget says, "As long as you spend no more than [insert amount], you'll have no problems," you can pay for your groceries or the kids' school clothes guilt-free, worry-free. You can do it with joy, even! One of the joys I have as a financial coach is witnessing the incredible feeling clients encounter the very first month they budget. It's important to realize that money stress doesn't stay in its own compartment. "Personal finance" isn't simply one part of your life. It transcends all areas of your life. Now, I don't mean that money is everything. What I mean is everything you do in life directly or indirectly involves money.

When money is good and you're on a budget, when everything is planned and accounted for, you don't stress about taking off work if your kid is sick, nor fixate on the fact your job no longer allows overtime.

However, when you're in a crisis and have no plan, it's hard to think about anything but money, right? When you drive a couple hours to see family, you're thinking about the cost of gas. When you're invited to brunch with your friends, you're anxious about how you'll pay for your waffles. When your child shows you their big toe poking through their sock, you're not giggling and enjoying the silly moment, you're worried about when you'll have the extra funds for new socks! This is why money problems wear us down so much. It finds its way into our good moments, spoiling them before they can happen.

I don't say this to sour the mood, but to point out what you're already feeling. Your current money situation has your whole life in its clutches. When your finances aren't in your control, it takes hold of everything and brings stress, anger, and fear with it. Money has stolen your joy, and worse, your time. Without a budget, your money is your dictator! When you're on a budget, you take back control of your own life, your own finances, and your own mental health. Take back what's yours. Don't fear the budget. Be empowered by it.

BUDGETING IS A LIFESTYLE

If you've budgeted before and it hasn't worked, let me ask you: Did you budget or did you log and track your expenses? Tracking your expenses is accounting, not budgeting. Totaling income and expenses at the end of the month is like driving down the highway at 70 mph, but instead of looking ahead through the windshield, you're looking back through the rear window. If this is how you drive your car, what is going to happen in less than five seconds? You're going to crash. This is what happens to our finances when we're only tracking our expenses. We crash. This isn't budgeting. Budgeting is proactive. You figure out how much everything is going to cost and how you're going to pay for it *before the month starts*.

Then, during the month, you ensure everything falls into place like you planned or adjust as needed.

Accounting, on the other hand, is reactive. It's looking back at what you've spent and organizes it into various categories. When you track expenses, you're not managing where your money goes. Your money is still doing what it wants, and you're made to watch and deal with it. When you track expenses, you still have no control and you're still stressed! Accounting isn't bad at all, it's just not helpful on its own without a budget.

Realizing a budget is proactive probably intimidates some of you because what this means is budgeting takes work and takes time. It's not something you set and forget; it's a lifestyle. All your transactions affect your budget, and because your spending (and maybe your income) changes from month to month, you should regularly consult your budget, adjust your budget, and track your budget. It evolves along with you.

Would it be great if you could set up a spreadsheet, load your transactions into it, and your finances would miraculously be resolved every month? Definitely! However, I'm sure you've tried that, and it didn't work. Even if your life is pretty predictable, it's not *completely* predictable. Some months you have car repairs, annual bills, birthday gifts, and plenty more that doesn't come up in other months, so when you don't plan for those things individually at the beginning of each month, you'll find you're still coming up short, you still feel controlled by your money, and you still can't get out of debt and reach your financial goals. In order to make your budget work this time, here are four key points, an overview of sound budgeting principles, that will help you succeed with your next budget. You will learn the actual step-by-step budgeting process in Chapter 6.

THE FOUR KEYS TO BUDGETING

1. Update It

Budgeting isn't a set-it-and-forget-it system. Budgeting needs to be a way of life for the rest of your life. Since your life changes regularly, your budget needs to be updated regularly too. Before the beginning of each month, you need to create a new budget for that month. For example, by March 31 you need to have April's budget complete. You actually have to sit and consider April, look at your calendar, recall past annual expenses, project your income, and plan accordingly.

Some months, it may not be additional expenses you plan for, but more income. Some months you'll have extra paychecks. Where's that money going? Whether you expected the income or not, realize that for a proper budget to work, each dollar needs to be accounted for. Your bonus paycheck isn't extra to spend. You need to find a place for it. If you have irregular income, this is even more important for you. You have to predict what your income will be, but once that paycheck hits your account, you need to update your budget and ensure all the money is accounted for. Whether you have extra, or you're short of what you planned, you need to adjust your budget accordingly. No matter your situation, updating your budget is essential to successfully following it.

2. Balance It

The budget we're going to make together in the next chapter is a "zero-based budget," which means you take your total income and subtract all your budget expense categories to get zero dollars. An expense category is not only for consumer spending, but could be for (a) putting money in savings, (b) paying off debt, or (c) investing in retirement, etc. Your budget balanced to zero is not a bad thing, it's actually the goal.

You want the balance to equal zero because it shows that each dollar went to its assigned spot. It also means that you won't have a false sense of security about overspending during the month. For example, if you have an "extra" $300 in your budget just floating there, you'll run into trouble. Let's say you go to the grocery store and spend a little over your budget. You'll say, "That's okay, I have that extra wiggle room budgeted in here." Then, you'll do the same thing at the gas station, the coffee shop, the department store, and on Amazon until you've spent that $300 two or three times over! When you keep a zero-based budget where each dollar has an assignment, you don't overspend and there's no surprises. Sometimes, things are unpredictable. I get it. Your income and expenses vary. Maybe you didn't make quite as much as you thought you would. Or maybe you were under budget in eating out and three other categories this month.

No matter the situation, you need to get that budget to zero. If you have extra money left over one month, decide where it will go. Do you put it in savings? Do you use it to pay off more debt? Depending on which Baby Step you're on, figure out the best place to put that extra cash. However, note that a zero-based budget does not mean your bank account should drop to zero. You need a few hundred dollars as a buffer to sit in your account, but it remains untouched and is not included in your zero-based budget.

If you have the opposite problem and more expenses than income, you need to cut out what you can to even it up. So, if the gas bill was more than you anticipated, but you still have $100 budgeted for eating out, see if shifting those numbers gets you to zero. If, after all the shifting and adapting, you still have too many expenses, find a way to quickly get more money, like selling a possession or getting a part-time job, and then alter your budget for next month to ensure this doesn't happen again.

Don't let that last scenario scare you. If you stick diligently to a budget, you won't encounter that problem too often, because you'll keep track of your transactions all month long, adjust as you go, and you won't be waiting until the end of the month to realize there's a big problem. When you encounter a budget issue mid-month, you'll be able to correct it.

3. Discuss It

If you're married, you both need to be involved in the budgeting process. One spouse might make the budget, but the other spouse must engage in the discussion and review process. One of the leading causes of divorce is lack of communication. A lack of communication around money usually means a lack of communication everywhere. Keynote speaker Jolene Brown says, "Without communication, cooperation, and commitment, you can only count on resistance, resentment, and revenge."[4] Isn't that the truth!

Now, if you are the spouse that assembles the budget, that does not make you king or queen of the hill—you are not supposed to be a dictator of your family's finances. Your spouse should ask questions, challenge certain areas, and ask you how they can best help. Glancing over it and saying,

"Looks good, babe," won't cut it. You both have to buy into and contribute to the final plan. (If you and your spouse are unicorns and enjoy assembling the budget together, by all means feel free to do that.)

Arrange for a weekly meeting to discuss your budget with your spouse. Once you get the hang of budgeting, you can drop this down to bi-weekly or even monthly. This step alone could change your finances, and, in turn, your marriage. I may not be a marriage counselor, but I've had many married couples come back to me after the first month of coaching and tell me how much better their relationship is now that they're communicating about money. Once they learn to talk about this difficult and stressful topic, they learn to communicate better about other difficult and stressful topics.

I will never forget one of the first married couples I ever worked with. In our first session, they told me they'd been fighting about money for all nineteen years of their marriage, starting the first night of their honeymoon. One month after sitting down to discuss their budget together with me, they both agreed they never had talked that much about their finances, and got along during those conversations, in their entire marriage. Another client called me fifteen minutes after their first session ended to share ecstatically, "The entire car ride home has been all about our finances, and we're already getting on the same page!"

Some of you reading this might be thinking, "That may have been easy for them, but you don't realize how bad my relationship is with my spouse. We're not in a good place at all right now." If this is you, and you're not confident these conversations will go well, or you and your spouse have been volatile around money discussions in the past, I strongly encourage you to talk with your pastor, a marriage counselor, and/or a financial coach.

This reminds me of a couple I coached who did just that. They shared during their last session with me some intimate details of how bad their relationship was that I wasn't initially aware of. While learning how to budget and communicate were some of their biggest takeaways, it was the results from those takeaways that were profound. Prior to meeting with me, they'd been talking seriously about getting a divorce. In fact, the wife also shared that early in our time working together, they were sleeping in separate bedrooms. That's how dire their relationship was.

Right after the wife shared that, the husband said with a smile across his face, "We aren't now!"

Before you get married, you'll need to be unified with how you're going to handle your finances as a couple. In fact, an article from FoundationsU[5] shares four areas marriage counselors say you need to be aligned with your future spouse on that can almost eliminate the possibility of divorce: religion, children, in-laws, and you guessed it . . . money. I strongly encourage you to go through some good pre-marital counseling and/or attend classes around these subjects, to give your upcoming marriage the best chance for success.

If you're single, you won't be dealing with these kinds of communication problems, and you'll have more power over your money because your choices won't need the approval of someone else. However, without a built-in accountability partner, you will have challenges. First, it can be easier to overspend, and second, if numbers and spreadsheets aren't your strong suit then it's easy to convince yourself to not create a budget. Having someone you can contact when you're unsure of a purchase or if you need help to review your budget for any gaps is very helpful. They may remind you about upcoming expenses or find miscalculations here and there. It's good to have someone in your corner that can help you feel extra confident about your budget.

I had a single client a few years ago that smartly set up accountability partners in multiple areas of her life so she always had someone to turn to. She has a physically demanding job and one day her back was sore, and she decided the soreness in her back warranted a massage. As she jumped on the website to book an appointment for the end of the day, she realized she was having an impulsive thought. So, she went to her accountability partner at work and asked if she should get the massage. Her accountability partner asked, "Is it in the budget?" It wasn't. In fact, it would have overdrawn her account. The simple conversation shook my client out of her impulsive thinking and reminded her a warm bath before bed would do just fine—and wouldn't cost her a thing.

Review your budget with someone. Discuss it thoroughly and make sure it'll work for you. I know this takes time, but remember, budgeting is a lifestyle. It has never worked for you in the past to set it and forget it or simply go back at the end of the month and play accountant, categorizing your purchases. The budget is a living, breathing document you have to care for.

4. Live It

Living out your budget will take some time to get used to. Usually, it's about three months of trying, adjusting, and trying again, to get the budgeting process down, and close to six months to a year to make it a habit. Don't get discouraged if the zero-based budget doesn't work for you the first time (or even the second time). Plus, you may still be overcoming some past trauma from financial failure. That Cycle of Regret can be intense, and it can leave you feeling defeated before you even start. Expect those big feelings, but don't expect them to stay around for long. After months of consulting the budget, discussing the budget, and tracking the budget, peace and confidence will charge you through the rest of the Pyramid.

One of my first clients was a single mom that had over $60,000 of consumer debt, minimal amount in savings, and did not have a working budget. When she hired me, she wanted to get on a budget and pay off her debt. She had no idea how to budget, especially when it came to non-monthly expenses like school supplies. Looking back, one of the biggest things she learned was how to be flexible with her budget. For example, if a twenty-dollar school field trip expense came up out of the blue, she reduced a different expense from her budget so she could pay for her child's field trip and not go over budget.

Like many of my clients, it took her ninety days to get the hang of budgeting. But once she did, I'm excited to report she paid off all her debt, including her mortgage, and retired early all in less than ten years. She would tell you that following the four keys to budgeting, **Update It**, **Balance It**, **Discuss It**, and **Live It**, were essential in achieving all her financial goals.

YOUR BUDGET IS THE KEY TO SUCCESS

Budgeting is the most important part of your financial success. No matter how much head knowledge you have about finances or how good you are with a calculator, you won't win with money until you master budgeting. So, in the next chapter, I'm going to show you how to make a budget, use a budget, and thrive on a budget. Once you conquer this step, you'll be on your way to financial success and ready to tackle the next hurdle.

Chapter 5 Takeaways

- **Don't wait!** Get on a budget now and set yourself up for future success. A budget gives you a sense of peace and control that you've been craving all your adult life.

- **A budget is nothing more than a strategic shopping list**. Budgets aren't something you do when things are tight or when you're poor. Millionaires became millionaires because they used budgets as tools to live on less than they made. Budgets are a way of planning and prioritizing what is important to you, so you get the most value from your money.

- **Budgeting is proactive.** Tracking expenses is important, but it's reactive. Budgeting happens *before* the month starts. You figure out how much everything is going to cost and how you're going to pay for it, and then during the month, you ensure everything falls into place like you planned or adjust as needed.

- **Follow the four keys to budgeting.** Update your budget a minimum of once per month. Balance your budget by using the zero-based budgeting method. If married, discuss your budget weekly with your spouse. If single, discuss your budget at least monthly with your accountability partner or financial coach. Live out your budget. Remember, budgeting is not a set-it-and-forget-it exercise, but a way of life for the rest of your life.

- **Your budget is the answer to winning with your money.** Budgeting is the most important part of your financial freedom journey. Budgeting as a lifestyle will bring you a sense of control and give you hope as you move toward your financial future.

CHAPTER 6

How Do I Make and Use a Budget?

By failing to prepare, you are preparing to fail.

—*Benjamin Franklin*

BUDGETING THE RIGHT WAY can literally change your life. Now that we've pushed away myths about budgeting to see the power of a plan, you can finally step out of the Cycle of Regret. On the Knowledge Level of the Pyramid, you get a taste of freedom the minute you start making and following a budget. Being intentional with your money will feel like you got an unexpected raise at work. A speaker at a recent financial conference shared that on average you gain $400 per month instantly just by getting organized with your finances. That's almost $5,000 extra a year! I bet that'll kick at least one debt out of the equation and give you a starter emergency fund.

Here's the thing, if you've thought budgeting didn't apply to you, or if you were accounting instead of budgeting, it's time to throw all that away and start fresh. I want you to get that raise! When you budget using the zero-based method, you'll have the best chance at success. I know this because not only have I used this method, but so have other money experts, millionaires, and people like you when they journeyed to financial freedom.

I worked with a couple once where the wife literally recoiled at the word *budget* as though I'd made her take a bite of raw chicken liver. She even said, "Don't ever use that word around me again!" That was awkward, considering I'm a financial coach. That's like telling a chef he can't say the word *recipe*. I treaded lightly for a while but still had her make a budget. Soon enough, she saw the power of her budget and gave me an apology.

On a frigid day in the depth of a Midwest winter, she admitted during a session that she was feeling down after weeks of being cooped up with little sunlight. I reminded her of her gardening fund she'd been putting money into all season. "Remember the spring you're going to have when it's time to spend that gardening fund! It's just around the corner!"

She smiled and said, "Thank you for reminding me of that. I feel so much better." We went on to discuss her plans for spring and summer landscaping since that year would be the first one where she could plant a garden and actually enjoy it, rather than stressing about the cost of supplies and time. Did you catch that? The budget went from a word that triggered anger and anxiety to a word that triggered hope and joy. That's what using a budget can do!

So, if you're ready to get control of your finances, let's begin making that budget. This is one of the most important tools, not only on the Knowledge Level, but for the entire Pyramid. If you can create a sustainable budgeting lifestyle, you will change your financial future. Suddenly everything will start to become possible.

Think back to Chapter 2 where you dreamed big about your future. Before we head into creating your budget, revisit some of those questions you asked yourself about your idyllic future, free of the financial burden you feel now. What do you want to do with your time and money? What do you want to see changed? What do you want to have? What do you want to give? Think back to the short- and long-term goals you set and understand that your ticket to your dreams is simply getting on a budget. I say "simply," but those of you who've tried and tried again to get your money in order know that it's not as easy as it looks—but you can get there with a few extra tools.

Okay, now that you've had a second to dream, let's reel it back to today. You're not going on big vacations and buying a vintage car just yet. Today, we're getting out of debt and saving up. You want peace and clear direction, right? Well, we can do that with an intentional budget and focused discipline. Let's break it down, one step at a time with our fictional couple John and Jane Doe.

STEP 1: PICK YOUR BUDGET TOOL

Before we start, it's important to decide where the budget is going to live. I don't endorse a specific platform, but you need to choose one. You can find some good starting templates online, but every budget will need to be personalized and expanded. Furthermore, let the tool work for you, not the other way around. If the tool or template isn't working, pick a new one, but don't expect to find something perfect. Also, I don't recommend using multiple tools. Keep it simple, keep going, and figure out how the tool can best work for you.

Whether you use a notebook and pen, a mobile app, a website on your computer, or spreadsheet software, in your chosen template, you need to factor in when you get paid, when bills are due, and list every expense as we discussed earlier. Each month, you'll create a new budget using your tool. Remember, from month to month your budget can change, so your system needs to be easy to regularly adjust.

STEP 2: LIST YOUR INCOME

Now that you have your tool, write down all your income. Do this by listing your monthly take-home pay, broken down by paychecks. The following page shows a sample record of John and Jane Doe's monthly incomes. You need to have enough in each pay period to cover the expenses for that week's bills. You'll want to include any money you get from side hustles or any other sources outside your regular paycheck. Remember, we're accounting for each dollar—no dollars left behind!

	INCOME				
Who	Jane	John	John		
Pay Date	1st	10th	25th		
Amount	$2,760	$1,700	$1,700	←	Take-Home Pay

If you have a variable income, you can still do this. Track your hours or sales and fill out your budget based on a conservative prediction. Review your pay periods for the upcoming month and make a realistic prediction of what your take-home pay will be for each check. For some people, this may be challenging at first, but once you have done it for ninety days, you'll be pleasantly surprised how close you can get to predicting your paychecks.

Even someone on a salary may get an unexpected bonus or get income from selling an asset. Each dollar must be planned for and assigned a job. This should be easy to do since your budget will be discussed and managed all month long. Part of the discussion process will be accounting for all your income and evaluating those paychecks. This is a zero-based budget, so each dollar must be budgeted regardless of when it comes into your account. As I said in the last chapter, budgeting is a way of life for the rest of your life.

STEP 3: LIST YOUR EXPENSES

The best way to discover what all your expenses are is by opening your bank and credit card statements and scrolling through every transaction. I know this may take a while, but if you look at the past thirty to ninety days of transactions, you'll find all your regular expenses. Once you have all those things written out, consider annual or irregular expenses too. Yearly memberships, car registration, salon appointments, and other similar costs are easy to forget, but must be included. Yes, even track that five-dollar bill you spend once a year so you can play that silly phone game ad-free. Sometimes we crush budgets and sometimes we crush candy.

Below is a sample spreadsheet of John and Jane Doe's expenses. You may have more expenses to add or fewer ones listed here.

EXPENSES

Categories	Amount	Due Date
GIVE		
Tithe to Church	$616	
Other Giving		
HOUSEHOLD		
Groceries	$1,200	
Paper Goods/Supplies	$100	
Clothing	$80	
Eating Out	$120	
Dr. Visits/Co-Pay	$100	
SHELTER		
Mortgage	$1,600	1st
Repairs/Upkeep		
UTILITIES		
Electric	$148	20th
Gas/Propane	$88	23rd
Water	$73	12th
Garbage	$20	16th
Cell Phone	$150	2nd
Internet	$89	5th
AUTO		
Auto Loan Payment	$490	5th
Fuel - Gasoline	$160	
Auto Maintenance	$75	
Auto Insurance	$212	12th
INSURANCE		
Life Insurance - John	$33	5th
Life Insurance - Jane	$19	5th
DISCRETIONARY		
Pocket Money	$60	
School Supplies	$25	
Subscriptions	$129	12th
Christmas	$100	
DEBT		
Student Loan	$157	2nd
Credit Card	$88	26th

When you're listing your expenses, leave no stone unturned. The more expenses you catch, the fewer surprises you'll have in those first ninety days when you're working out how to set up and manage your budget. If any of your bills have a regular due date, jot that down too, as that'll be important for later steps.

STEP 4: LIST YOUR DEBTS

You arranged your debts in order of lowest to highest balance back in Chapter 4, so hopefully this information is still handy. Having these numbers is essential for completing the Knowledge Level. If you weren't thorough enough when you did this earlier (or you were too scared to do it), go ahead and look up all your debts. If these numbers really freak you out, try to do this part with someone who can support you and encourage you. There's nothing to be ashamed of. You're taking the right steps to fix this, so breathe, forgive yourself, and use this as fuel to stick with the budget and the future challenges of reaching your financial goals.

Once all your debts are totaled, include the minimum payments in your list of expenses. Keep the totals handy so you can see how your debt snowball is knocking down one debt at a time.

STEP 5: SAVE WITH SINKING FUNDS

Unexpected expenses often throw off budgets. We call them unexpected, but are they really? We may not know when, but we know that someday we'll need to hire a plumber, visit urgent care, or buy our kids new pairs of shoes. So we'll want to insert savings plans for these expenses that come up throughout the year, but are not monthly. These savings plans are called "sinking funds." Typically, sinking funds are used for things like saving for big purchases like a car replacement or vacation. However, you can use the sinking fund principle to save for non-monthly expenses like holidays, car repairs, school supplies, etc. You save money every month toward them, so

SINKING FUND TRACKER

ITEMS TO SAVE FOR	AMOUNT NEEDED	÷ MONTHS	= MONTHY BUDGETED	BALANCE	SAVE BY
Doctor Visits/Co-pays	$1,200	12	$100	$500	N/A
Auto Insurance	$1,272	6	$212	$848	Apr & Nov
School Supplies	$300	12	$25	$200	Aug
Car Repairs	$900	12	$75	$300	N/A
Christmas	$1,200	12	$100	$800	Dec

Here's how a sinking fund works: You take the total amount you need to save and divide it by the number of months you have to save for it. Whatever that number is, that's what you save every month either in a separate bank account or in an envelope system. For example: Let's say you spend $1,200 per year on Christmas. I'm not only talking about the gifts you purchase for your immediate family. You have to include other expenses like fuel to travel to grandma's house, food for hosting, wrapping paper and wrapping supplies, decor, Christmas cards, company grab bags, and anything else you spend money on for the holidays. If you're starting your sinking fund in January, take $1,200 and divide it by twelve months, and that equals $100 per month you'll need to save. If you're starting your sinking fund in July, then take $1,200 divided by six months, and you'll need to save $200 each month until December. You will need to do this exercise for all your non-monthly expenses. Think about this: Next time the car needs tires, the money will be there. You won't need to pull anything from your emergency fund. You won't need to break the budget, and you definitely won't need to stress—because you've got the necessary money in a sinking fund! So, spend some time brainstorming these sorts of expenses. If you are having trouble determining what to consider saving for in a sinking fund, use the list on the following page.

SINKING FUND EXAMPLES

Doctor Visits/Co-pays	Birthdays/Other Gifts
Glasses/Contacts	School Supplies
Insurance (Home, Renters, Auto, Life)	Travel/Vacation
Home Repairs/Upkeep	Vet Expenses
Car Registrations	Tuition
Car Repairs	Annual Memberships/Subscriptions
Christmas	Hobbies

Once you determine what sinking funds you're going to save for and include the data in your budgeting spreadsheet or app, you can either use a bank account to save for these items or you can use cash envelopes. If you're going to use envelopes for your sinking funds, I would not recommend carrying those specific envelopes with you everywhere you go. That would not be wise. If you decide to use a bank account, I recommend keeping track of all your sinking funds, whether in a separate spreadsheet or app or inside your chosen budget template, and only use one bank account. You don't need to open separate bank accounts for each sinking fund. I mean . . . you could . . . but depending on how many sinking funds you create, you could have a lot of bank accounts to reconcile.

At this point, you might be getting a little overwhelmed by everything you're totaling up. It might even be adding up to be more than your monthly pay. This is probably why budgeting hasn't worked for you in the past. Your previous budgets weren't specific or thorough enough and may not have truly included all your expenses. For now, don't worry about the high total. Just get it all down, and we'll work through budgeting problems and how to solve them in the next chapter. Hang tight!

STEP 6: DETERMINE YOUR CURRENT GOAL

Back in Chapter 4, we discussed the first three Baby Steps. If you're beginning Baby Step 1, you'll need to save for your starter emergency fund, so include it somewhere on your list of expenses. However, if you're on Baby Step 2 (the debt snowball) and you already have your emergency fund, your extra income is going to be focused on your smallest debt first.

STEP 7: RECORD WHEN EVERYTHING GETS PAID—INCLUDING YOURSELF

Your budget includes all your paydays and the due dates on your bills, right? Now make sure those things balance out. Total up your expenses for each weekly or biweekly period, depending on how often you get paid. Then, determine if that number is less than your total weekly or bi-weekly income. That's what we want. Your paycheck should cover all the bills for that pay period. That means you need to know every bill's due date. I meet with many clients who have no idea when their autopay bills come out. When you look back at your previous transactions from your bank statement(s) to make your budget, this information is going to be crucial. Your bills can't exceed the income you bring in each pay period—otherwise you won't be able to cover those costs and you'll have overdrafts. On the following page is Jane Doe's contribution from her paycheck toward the household expenses. (The full budget and allocations from both the husband and wife's paychecks can be found after Step 8.)

PAYCHECK DISTRIBUTION

Categories	Amount	Due Date	Who	Jane	
			Pay Date	1st	
			Amount	$2,760	
GIVE					
Tithe to Church	$616			$276	
Other Giving					
HOUSEHOLD					
Groceries	$1,200				
Paper Goods/Supplies	$100				
Clothing	$80				
Eating Out	$120			$120	
Dr. Visits/Co-Pay	$100			$100	
SHELTER					
Mortgage	$1,600	1st		$1,600	
Repairs/Upkeep					
UTILITIES					
Electric	$148	20th			
Gas/Propane	$88	23rd			
Water	$73	12th			
Garbage	$20	16th			
Cell Phone	$150	2nd		$150	
Internet	$89	5th		$89	
AUTO					
Auto Loan Payment	$490	5th			
Fuel - Gasoline	$160				
Auto Maintenance	$75			$75	
Auto Insurance	$212	12th			
INSURANCE					
Life Insurance - John	$33	5th		$33	
Life Insurance - Jane	$19	5th		$19	
DISCRETIONARY					
Pocket Money	$60				
School Supplies	$25				
Subscriptions	$129	12th			
Christmas	$100			$100	
DEBT					
Student Loan	$157	2nd		$157	
Credit Card	$88	26th			
BABY STEP GOAL					
Pay Off Debt	$228			$41	
TOTAL (INCOME-EXPENSES=ZERO)				$0	

Too many expenses on one paycheck is likely a reason your account is getting overdrawn each month. If you find your expenses are higher than the income for that period, you may have to make a few calls to change your due dates on bills that allow you to (most companies will), so you can spread out your expenses to fit how and when you get paid. Taking time to move these expenses around and determine where the problems are will save you a lot of headaches.

STEP 8: ASSEMBLE YOUR BUDGET

This is where you're going to put all the information you have gathered, and assemble your budget. If you haven't already, you'll need to determine which budgeting tool you're going to use. With your chosen tool, you're going to include all your income, expenses, debts, and sinking funds. Everything has to be included. Be sure to add due dates for all your bills so you are able to pay them on time. Throughout the month, if anything new comes up you forgot to plan for, add it right away to the budget and adjust accordingly. Hopefully, by the end of a three-month period of budgeting, there will be little to no surprises.

As mentioned in Chapter 5, determine which day and time of the week you'll check in with your spouse or accountability partner and add it to your calendar. When it's scheduled on your calendar, for example, Mondays at 8 p.m. or Saturdays at 9 a.m., you'll be less likely to skip it or try to handle every hiccup on your own. Discuss your budget thoroughly with your spouse or accountability partner to keep everything balanced before a potential problem occurs. No more overdraft fees! No more unpaid bills! It all ends with keeping a budget.

EXPENSES

Categories	Amount	Due Date
GIVE		
Tithe to Church	$616	
Other Giving		
HOUSEHOLD		
Groceries	$1,200	
Paper Goods/Supplies	$100	
Clothing	$80	
Eating Out	$120	
Dr. Visits/Co-Pay	$100	
SHELTER		
Mortgage	$1,600	1st
Repairs/Upkeep		
UTILITIES		
Electric	$148	20th
Gas/Propane	$88	23rd
Water	$73	12th
Garbage	$20	16th
Cell Phone	$150	2nd
Internet	$89	5th
AUTO		
Auto Loan Payment	$490	5th
Fuel - Gasoline	$160	
Auto Maintenance	$75	
Auto Insurance	$212	12th
INSURANCE		
Life Insurance - John	$33	5th
Life Insurance - Jane	$19	5th
DISCRETIONARY		
Pocket Money	$60	
School Supplies	$25	
Subscriptions	$129	12th
Christmas	$100	
DEBT		
Student Loan	$157	2nd
Credit Card	$88	26th
BABY STEP GOAL		
Pay Off Debt	$228	
TOTAL (INCOME-EXPENSES = ZERO)		

INCOME

Who	Jane	John	John	
Pay Date	1st	10th	25th	
Amount	$2,760	$1,700	$1,700	
	$276	$170	$170	
		$600	$600	
		$50	$50	
			$80	
	$120			
	$100			
	$1600			
		$148		
		$88		
		$73		
		$20		
	$150			
	$89			
			$490	
		$80	$80	
	$75			
		$212		
	$33			
	$19			
			$60	
			$25	
		$129		
	$100			
	$157			
			$88	
	$41	$130	$57	
	$0	$0	$0	

STEP 9: BALANCE YOUR BUDGET

Now that you have all the numbers down in one organized location, the last thing you need to do is balance your budget to zero. As mentioned before, that doesn't mean your bank account should be at zero. If you have $500 left over after adding in all your numbers, determine where you want the $500 to go. Do not call the $500 cushion, pad, or miscellaneous. If you don't give the $500 a name, you may spend $800 wondering where the $500 went. Another way of looking at this is if you have kids or lead a team at work, you wouldn't manage 80 percent of your team and let the other 20 percent do whatever they wanted. Instead, every child or every team member would have an assignment. The same is true for your money. Conversely, if you tally everything up, and you're $500 short in your budget, you will have to go back and reduce or eliminate some expenses to get your budget to balance. This goes back to the principle of living on less than you make.

Once you have balanced your budget for the month, you'll need to balance each pay period to zero. This may seem like a tedious step. However, I see a lot of people do this in their heads already. All I'm asking you to do is to be intentional and determine which paychecks cover which expenses, and make sure each paycheck balances, that is, your paycheck minus your expenses should equal zero.

Once everything is accounted for and your budget is balanced, you now have a road map you can follow. With this budget you will feel a sense of hope and empowerment that will give you the fuel you need to reach your goals.

STEP 10: EDIT YOUR BUDGET AS NEEDED

As I mentioned in the last chapter, budgeting is not a set-it-and-forget-it tool. Your budget needs to be updated whenever changes occur. This can happen both on the income side and the expense side of the budget.

I often hear wage earners don't budget because each pay period is different and they reason that you can't budget without a predictable income. The reality is these people need to be on a budget as much, if not more, than someone who can predict their income.

Let's go back to John Doe. He's a wage earner making $30 per hour and is paid bi-weekly (every other week). He never works the same amount of hours. Some paychecks he works a little less than full-time hours and other paychecks he has overtime included. John can predict with some accuracy that in the next two weeks he's going to work seventy hours. When John works seventy hours in a given pay period, he knows his paycheck will be roughly $1,700 after taxes and benefits. So for budgeting purposes, John would put $1,700 on the income column.

Friday is payday, and his paycheck was actually $1,800 because he worked extra hours during this pay period. Before spending any of his paycheck, he would need to go back to the budget, change the income to $1,800 and determine where the additional $100 is going to go.

BUDGET EDITING EXAMPLE

				Who	John	John
				Pay Date	10th	10th
Categories	Amount	Due Date		Amount	$1,700	$1,800
GIVE	Updated					
Tithe to Church	$626				$170 → $180
UTILITIES	Updated					
Electric	$198	20th			$148 → $198
BABY STEP GOAL	Updated					
Pay Off Debt	$268				$130 → $170
TOTAL (INCOME-EXPENSES=ZERO)					$0	$0

Jane's contributions stayed the same for all categories this month, but since John's income changed, they adjusted for that by adding $10 more to tithing. They also found out their electric bill was $50 higher than previously estimated, but because of his higher paycheck, they didn't have to find other ways within the budget to cover it. And with $40 left over, they put that extra $40 toward their debt.

Once his budget is balanced, he can now live on his budget based on his most recent changes. John would do the same thing if the reverse happened and his actual paycheck was $1,600 because he worked fewer hours. He would need to edit the income portion of the budget and then reduce $100 worth of expenses before spending his paycheck.

The same rule applies to expenses. Let's say your utility bills fluctuate every month because you're not on budget billing.[1] Each month when you create a new budget, you will estimate how much each utility bill will be. Then when your actual utility bills come in, before paying your bills, you will edit the budget with the actual information. Let's say John Doe budgeted $250 for one of his utility bills and when the actual bill came in, it was $300. John would first go to the budget and raise that bill to $300. He would then need to find other expenses in the budget that he can reduce by $50 to make the budget balance. He may be able to adjust one expense, or he may need to adjust multiple expenses to balance the budget. Either way, you edit the budget first, then you pay your bills. You would do the same thing for any other expenses that you're unsure of what the actual bill is going to be.

This may seem a little overwhelming. But the good news is this adjusting and balancing doesn't take long. Once you get the hang of reviewing and editing your budget prior to spending your paycheck, it will only take a matter of minutes to do. And those few extra minutes you invest in editing your budget will save you hours of headaches later trying to figure out where all your money went.

GET CONTROL OF SPENDING

Your budget is all ready to go. It's time to start putting all this to work. But I know what you're thinking. "Justin, I've tried budgets plenty of times. The idea is great, but I can't stop spending!" This is where a lot of my clients get hung up before they start working with me. They set a max spending limit for themselves on paper, and then they blow right past it. We can't do this anymore, remember? Because our budgets are zero-based, that means each dollar spent over the limit will make your budget off-balance.

When people overspend, they usually do one of two things. They either panic and start shuffling things around to make up for the overspending, but keep overspending and making more problems until there's nowhere else to shuffle money from. Or they give up and declare they'll try budgeting next month. They try again the next month and nothing changes—yep, that's the Cycle of Regret.

You know that it's time to try something different to stop overspending. What could that be? Pay with cash. Yes, that's right, cash. Believe it or not, you can still make quite a lot of purchases using cash!

THE CASH-ENVELOPE SYSTEM

One of the best ways to keep a budget is to make it harder for you to spend money. Studies show that people spend up to 18 percent more when they pay with debit or credit cards versus paying with cash.[2] Our brains don't feel the loss of money as harshly when we use a credit card. Plus, credit cards allow for ignorance. You can keep yourself blissfully unaware of how much money you have (or don't have) when you're swiping a card and hoping for the best. With cash, you're always made aware of exactly how much you have. If you only have twenty dollars and the item costs thirty dollars, you're not getting it. With a card, you might push it, especially if you have overdraft protection or a credit line.

So, you need to get an envelope wallet or some similar organization system. Each pay period, you'll withdraw cash from the bank or ATM for all the budget line items that are not automatically taken from your account. For example, you might not need an cash envelope for your electric bill or rent, but you do need one for groceries and clothing. If you're not sure what other types of expenses you might need for cash envelopes, the chart on the following page is a quick guide.

CASH ENVELOPE EXAMPLES

Groceries	Medications/Supplements
Eating Out	Hair & Personal Care
Paper Goods/Supplies	Pocket Money
Clothing	Babysitting
Date Night	Pet Supplies
Work Lunch	Additional Giving
Kids Sports/Activities	Hobbies

The envelopes of cash will keep your family accountable to stay under your limit. If you're worried about carrying so much cash around all the time, don't worry. I am not suggesting you carry around your entire wallet of money! Keep your wallet in a secure place and only pull out the money you need for that trip. If you're going grocery shopping, you don't need to be carrying around Christmas cash or the car-maintenance fund. This is another guardrail to keep you from overspending. I even recommend people have two envelope wallets. One for ongoing savings for repairs and whatnot and another for everyday spending.

That being said, there is a place for debit cards. When you make online purchases, rent a car, reserve a hotel, or travel internationally a debit card is essential. And yes, you can do those things with a debit card instead of a credit card. (My wife and I have used a debit card in each of these instances.) The goal is simply to opt for cash as often as possible because it's another layer of accountability.

Let's say you're buying Christmas gifts on Amazon, obviously you can't shove cash through the computer, but your Christmas savings is in an envelope. So what do you do? You put the cash needed (and previously budgeted) in the bank or ATM, then you fill your online cart and pay with your debit card. Is it inconvenient? Absolutely. That's the point. That's what makes cash such an ideal complement to budgeting.

I know that cooled some of your concerns, but I also know there are some of you out there still nervous about using cash. I have clients, often younger ones, who don't trust themselves with cash. They tell me, "Justin, any time I get cash from tips or from gifts, I spend it faster than any other money that I get!" They explain to me that since spending the money doesn't lower their bank account balance, they don't feel like it counts. No matter how much it is, they burn through it in a couple days and don't really feel the sting of spending it.

Not trusting yourself with cash is a valid concern, and it's good that you know your weaknesses well enough to plan for them. However, when I push my clients to try the combination of the cash envelopes with the budget, it works. It's the combo that's important. Cash alone is dangerous. A budget alone is incomplete. But together? Together, they're beautiful! The cash you had before didn't have an assignment, which is why it was so easy to spend. The money in your cash envelope system will have a plan before it gets into your hands, so you won't overspend.

There are apps that have modernized the envelope system if you really want to go digital. But it's my recommendation that you go old school with cash for ninety days. I've found that for most people, when they give the cash system a try, paying with cash for ninety days, they end up preferring it. But if you still don't like using cash after ninety days, go ahead and try a digital version of the cash envelope system.

DOES ALL THIS REALLY WORK?

I was a bit skeptical about this process too. But I'll never forget when we were in the thick of our debt-free journey, I was headed home really late one night from work, and I hadn't eaten yet. Normally I was home for supper, because family meals are really important to me, but on this day, duty called, and I worked extra hours. On my way home, I was ravenously hungry and wanted food stat!

The route I took back to my house was lined with big name fast-food chains, and the scent of those freshly made fries and juicy burgers was wafting in through my air vents. My stomach was rumbling, and I'd worked hard that day, so I decided I was going to "treat myself" for supper at one of the fast-food joints; however, the cash envelope for eating out was at home.

I rushed back to the house while I was assembling my order in my head: *Triple cheeseburger, large fries, large Pepsi, and chocolate chip cookies* (for the kids, of course). When I got home, everyone was in bed, and I hustled over to the wallet and eagerly opened the Eating Out envelope. To my horror there was no cash left in it! This was a problem, because I was still hungry, and I wouldn't get paid again until Friday.

With little self-control, and that triple cheeseburger clouding my judgment, I started looking through other envelopes to find some extra I could swap for my fast-food cravings. Finally, I found a hefty amount of "extra" cash in my home repair envelope, so I pulled out a crisp twenty-dollar bill and motioned to put it in my pocket—but a storm brewed in my mind. I knew I'd be cheating our home repair savings if I ate out. But I swore to myself it'd only be this one time, right?

I headed for the door and grabbed the doorknob. Conviction was looming over me, but I really wanted that food. After a moment, I released the doorknob and walked over to my recliner and sat down for a moment to contemplate my decision. (Wow, what a ridiculous amount of energy for some "convenient" food.) Though I knew that spending the money wouldn't send my family into financial hardship, I also knew it wouldn't reinforce our shared financial goals.

Ultimately, I decided to put the cash back where it belonged in the home-repair savings envelope. I ate leftovers instead and let myself fall into a grumpy mood. I went to bed feeling sorry for myself, but the next morning I thought, *How silly to get so worked up over something so trivial*. If I'd have gotten my triple cheeseburger, I'd have had serious buyer's remorse and shame. There were no regrets about eating leftovers. Instead, I was proud of myself and ready to tackle another day.

This is the power of the cash-envelope system. Having to go home and consult my envelopes created a barrier between me and the fast-food joint. It set up a guardrail keeping me on track toward my financial goals, rather than veering me off the path when I saw those golden arches. I truly can't tell you how many times my cash envelopes saved me like this. The cash-envelope system was one of the key components to keeping me focused all the way to the Freedom Level.

YOUR BUDGET IS YOUR KEY TO FREEDOM

If you follow your budget, it'll be one of the essential pieces of your success story. When you have control over where your money goes, your goals quickly materialize right in front of you. Suddenly, that hope of saving $1,000 can be mapped week by week until you accomplish that objective. Suddenly, buying Christmas presents doesn't feel so intimidating because the money is there. This budget, when followed correctly, will one thousand percent make you feel like you got a raise, like things are finally working in your favor. It's an incredible feeling.

However, possessing the knowledge of what your budget looks like and how to follow it isn't enough for everyone, and many of my clients end up in a Cycle of Regret after penciling out their first budget. Remember to give yourself ninety days to figure out your budget. There's a lot that can and will go wrong in those first three months, so prepare for it and stay focused. Then, let the rest of the Pyramid help you establish accountability and generate momentum to ride your budget all the way to financial freedom. What are we waiting for? Let's assemble the rest of the plan and find that peace of mind only a good budget can provide.

Chapter 6 Takeaways

- **Budgeting saves you money.** By creating and living on a budget, you could uncover on average $5,000 per year.

- **Select a budgeting tool: spreadsheet software, mobile app, printed template, or a simple notebook and pen**. Remember not to be a slave to the tool. The tool works for you. Once you have selected the tool, use the ten-step process of building your first budget.

- **The cash-envelope system is a great way to get control of your impulse spending.** Choose which line items in your budget you will use cash for (i.e., groceries, eating out, personal spending money, etc).

- **Debit cards work!** When you make online purchases, rent a car, reserve a hotel, or travel internationally, a debit card is essential. You can do the same things with a debit card you have been doing with a credit card.

- **Following your budget and using the cash-envelope system is a powerful combination.** The cash you had before didn't have an assignment, which is why it was so easy to spend. Now the money in your cash-envelope system has a plan, so you won't overspend.

LEVEL THREE

Commitment

CHAPTER 7

Putting It All Together

Whether you believe you can do a thing or not, you are right.

—*Henry Ford*

WE'VE WORKED THROUGH the Knowledge Level together, and now you have the tools, principles, and systems to change your financial future. Not only do you know exactly how you can win with your money and reach your goals, you've also learned to not be fooled by debt, selfish attitudes, and societal norms. On the Commitment Level, you will put this information together and apply it. These huge strides in your financial journey will pay off immensely. But I can still hear you ask, "How much will it pay off?"

The faster you work through the early levels of the Financial Freedom Pyramid, the more quickly you'll launch into that idyllic period of life where you don't owe any money and your bank account is stocked with emergency cash. Now, ask yourself, *Is it worth it?* Is it worth going through all the trouble to get to this state of financial freedom? Absolutely.

When you created your budget in the previous chapter, what you did was write down your *current* spending in each category. But you haven't challenged yourself to change your spending habits yet, and you must. If you continue to spend like you're spending, budgeting won't move any cash toward debt or savings. Before you can get to that point of financial security and peace, you need to have all debt (except your house) gone and your savings fully stocked. So how do we get there? Let's take the example situation below and figure out how this hypothetical client can pay down their debt quickly.

Shawn and Samantha make $90,000 a year and have $60,000 in debt. They aren't behind on any payments, but have no money in savings and are paying the minimum amounts on all their debts. If they continue this way, they'll get out of debt in twenty years.

Ouch, their situation is bleak. Shawn and Samantha have an above-average income, yet they won't be debt-free for twenty years! Back in Chapters 3 and 5, we talked about how people can be led by an attitude of what they *deserve*. Well, you owe it to yourself to empower your paycheck to do more than pay off creditors. To get out of the hole you've dug for yourself, you've got to get dirty and get to work. Below is what will happen if they adjust their budget:

Shawn and Samantha commit to using the debt snowball method which reduces their debt-free timeline to ten years. That's half the time! In addition to that, they start cutting expenses in their budget and living more intentionally. After reducing their grocery bill, committing to only eating at home, canceling their gym member-ships, going to home-brewed coffee, and a few other things, like finding less expensive auto and home insurance policies, Shawn and Samantha freed up $750 in their budget. This will take their get-out-of-debt journey from a ten-year trudge to a four-year hike.

That's looking better, right? But I know some of you have been at this for a while. You know that those extra years in debt mean more fatigue, more stress, and more interest payments. You're ready to be done with it, and four years isn't good enough. The thought of a financial coach saying,

"Just hang on for four more grueling years," makes you mad. Keep that anger and frustration. We need it to fuel you for the next scenario.

Shawn and Samantha weren't happy with those numbers, so Shawn got a second job and was able to consistently make an extra $500 a month (sometimes more). This reduced their debt-free journey by one more year. Finally, they'd be debt-free in three years. Still, that wasn't quite satisfying, so Samantha started a side-hustle,[1] and they cut down even more on their budget, so they had a total of $2,000 extra to go toward debt. Now, Shawn and Samantha would be out of debt in two years.

That looks even better, doesn't it? If you're not convinced, think back to an event that happened two or three years ago. Seems like it was yesterday, right? Time flies when you're having fun. Well, I can't say this debt-reduction journey will be fun, but it can be fast! Remember that the bigger commitment you make now, the shorter the pain will last. Yes, there's going to be some pain in this process—but have hope. Even if your situation looks different from this couple's, all these principles will work the same for you.

So, let's examine the current state of your budget, and see where you can make more or spend less. Like Shawn and Samantha, we want to find as much extra money as we can to go toward debt and/or savings.

IS YOUR BUDGET BALANCED?

To figure out how your budget can help you reach your goals, you first need to see if the budget is working for you. Don't be surprised if it's not. To figure this out, add up all your income and then subtract all your expenses, which includes all the non-monthly expenses, those unexpected expenses we've talked about in previous chapters. When you finish tallying your budget, you will discover one of three things: (1) It's balanced, but you still have questions, (2) it's not as bad as you thought, but you still wonder, *Where did all my money go?* or (3) it's worse than you thought, which is a hard but needed wake-up call. I'll help you determine what to do in every situation, so don't get overwhelmed by what you discover.

"I'm in the green. I've got extra!"

If you finished your budget and you have leftover income, that's great! This is a beautiful problem to have. That means you already have some wiggle room to hit those debt and savings goals early on. Refer back to the Baby Step you're on and throw all your extra money toward that. Put those dollars to work by paying down debt or filling up that savings account. Yes, you read that right, the "extra" money doesn't go to fancy restaurants, hobby supplies, vacations, and it for sure doesn't go toward a $2,000 gym membership. (Yeah, I'm never going to be able to let that go.) These additional dollars need to reinforce whatever your current money goals are. If you find an extra five dollars, that five dollars, depending on what Baby Step you're on, should either go toward your $1,000 emergency fund, your debt balance, or your three-to-six month living expenses fund.

"I'm in the red, but I can make a few cuts and make it green."

If after totaling up everything, you realize you're a few hundred or so short of having a zero-based budget, tighten up the budget a bit more to give yourself margin to get out of debt and to establish that emergency fund. It may be time to cut some subscriptions and switch to generic brand ketchup.

You'll be surprised how much you can save by making small, painless cuts in your budget. The average person spends $219 per month on subscriptions.[2] I doubt many of those are a necessity. Get rid of as much as possible. And what about eating out? The average household spends $166 per week going out to eat.[3] That means the average family of four is spending $664 a month! That's not necessary either, so cut that down as close to zero as possible. I'm sure you have plenty in your grocery cart every week that doesn't need to be there (and don't get me started on daily coffee runs or stops at the convenience store for energy drinks and sodas!). The point is if you're a little in the red, make small changes like this to get it back in the green. If you're already in the green, challenge yourself to get more in the green. The more extra you have, the better and faster it'll be for completing your next goal.

"I'm in the red, and I'll have to make significant cuts to get it in the green."

This one can be really stressful when you discover it, but isn't as bleak as you think. (Don't forget my wife and I were $700 in the red when I first looked into our financial predicament.) You'll need to start with reducing your lifestyle expenses, but you may also need to sell an asset or find additional ways to make more money.

After working with one client named Rafael, we realized he was $1,000 short paying his bills every month. Whoa! We combed through and found obvious places to cut but were still $200 short. That's not too far off, but obviously the $200 would not materialize out of thin air. So, I challenged Rafael to show me where he could cut even more in his budget.

He gave a quick, irritated sigh, and said, "Well, it looks like the only thing left is CrossFit, so I guess I'll cut that." This was a big step for him. I was really proud of him because the CrossFit® community is really tight-knit and loyal to their gyms. Leaving is not easy for people who are passionate about this hobby; however, Rafael saw his need and realized staying wasn't helping him reach his financial goals. Instead, he started working out using online videos at home. This is what the Commitment Level is all about!

Rafael now had a balanced budget, but that wasn't enough to accelerate his debt-free goals. (His situation looked a lot like Shawn and Samantha's did in the beginning, with a twenty-year plus debt-payoff projection.) Balancing Rafael's budget only got him covering all his expenses. We needed to do more to power through the three Baby Steps and gain enough momentum to reach financial freedom. He needed an additional $500 a month to pay off his $47,000 of debt in his goal time of two and a half years. In one of our sessions, I came to him with another painful suggestion. "Rafael, why not sell the car?" The payment on his luxury sedan was just under $500 a month, so there was his extra money for paying off his debt. Plus, if he sold the car, that would take care of $21,000 in auto loans as well.

"Absolutely not!" he said. "That is my dream car, and I am not selling it."

I acknowledged his concern, but offered another solution, "Then, if you are serious about getting out of debt, you'll need a second job." He wanted to keep his car, so he got that second job. Within a short period of time, he was making enough at this second job to pay his debt off faster than his original goal. He even earned enough to get back into his CrossFit gym. It was a huge success! However, without his initial sacrifices, he would never be where he is today—debt-free, with a full emergency fund, living his CrossFit life. How did he get there? Despite being in the red, he looked at his priorities, made sacrifices, and came out on top with a true win-win scenario. Even with awareness of his money situation and knowledge of sound financial principles, Rafael wouldn't have gotten anywhere without commitment.

"I'm way in the red, and it doesn't seem like there's a way out."
When you can't make enough cuts to get out of the red, it feels like you're in an apocalyptic scenario. Normally, this occurs when there are high amounts of credit card debt, student loans, and huge car payments. Since you can't cut required monthly payments, you feel totally stuck and overwhelmed. Hold onto hope, though, because many people in similar situations as yours have followed the Pyramid and gotten out of debt. It's tough, I won't lie, but you don't need a certain personality type or skill set to get through it. You've just got to be committed to the process.

I had clients from a small, rural town who were in a real financial bind. This couple was almost $100,000 in debt, not including their house. When I added up all their debt payments alone, it was $2,200 a month. That's $26,000 a year going to creditors! They were searching and grasping for anything real to pull them out of the hole but couldn't find any. Actually, it wasn't a hole, it was an abyss. To make matters worse, some of the money owed was to a family member, and they were ready to be paid back. The three of us started by going through the same process you have since Chapter 1:

1. They became **aware** of their situation.
2. They gained **knowledge** about money management principles.
3. Together we made a functional budget, and they were ready to **commit** at all costs.

Like you, they were feeling confident up to this point. They were finally hearing something new they could hold onto, or at least communicated in a way that felt approachable. However, their budget was in the red. *Way* in the red. They were almost $2,500 short every single month. (Feel free to gasp. It's warranted.)

After I quickly helped them find areas to cut to make more margin, they still remained $1,800 in the red per month. Unfortunately, it wasn't the only thing red. When I looked up, their faces were a ripe scarlet color, fear and shame overwhelmed them. Their mouths hung open and tears streamed down their faces. The wife said, "What can we do? We won't file for bankruptcy—we need another way out."

I had to pause and take a deep breath as I worked it all out in my mind. I shared with them the best prescription: "If you want to avoid bankruptcy and pay off all your debt, you need two to three extra jobs, and you'll have to sell everything you have. I mean everything, whether it brings in five dollars or five hundred."

Then, I broke the news that it would take five years. It would be five years of working, five years of spending nothing extra, five years of selling anything that wasn't nailed down. Truly, it'd be five years of misery…but the alternative was a lifetime of misery. That sounds intense and melodramatic, but it's true. Their situation was so dire, it truly was a circumstance of "choose your hard." In this instance, it was choose your *really* hard.

They decided to get on that long, hard road to freedom. They started discussing with eagerness what they'd sell and where they could further cut the budget down. However, finding extra jobs caused a lot of anxiety. You see, when you live in a metropolitan area, finding additional work is easy. There are help wanted signs everywhere, but in rural communities, there are very few available part-time jobs. The ones you do find are pretty much the worst of the worst. (Think *Dirty Jobs*,[4] but at minimum wage.)

When they exited my session that day, their heads were hanging low. I really hated that, because I always want my clients to leave with hope, like I want you to finish each chapter with hope. When we met again a month later, I found myself subconsciously holding my breath. I was prepared for a bleak outlook and bad news. However, I was surprised when the wife exclaimed, "I got two extra jobs!" The husband added, "And I'm at home after work every night putting something up for sale on Facebook Marketplace." Wow! Those were big steps. Over the next few months of sessions, they added more jobs and sold more possessions. Their house must have been a shell with a couple lawn chairs by the end of this. The husband even sold some big-kid toys that must have been pretty painful to let go of. Eventually, the couple was able to get in the green and push $500 a month toward debt.

They kept grinding and finding more ways to save money, and making money became like a game. Of course, it was hard. It was *really* hard to say no to everything for so long, but they'd tell you it was all worth it, because in six months they went from being behind by $2,500 every month to paying off over $25,000 in debt. With commitment to the plan, it only took that first month for their hope and their motivation to grow as they experienced progress.

Where are they now? They're still working on that debt snowball, but guess what? They're so close to freedom, and they tell me every time I see them it gets easier every month and the time really does fly. They feel a tremendous weight lifted off their shoulders, and they find joy in correcting their past mistakes and defining a new future. Truly, they've conquered their past shame and guilt and only have a little longer to go before all their future goals are realized. That gives me joy.

Now that we're on the Commitment Level, it's time to take your awareness of your situation and the knowledge of how to fix it to the next level with perseverance, accountability, and sacrifice. Knowing what needs to change is good, but you have to pursue that change at all costs.

COMMITMENT IS WORTH IT

I want to share one more story with you. Luke and Dianne finished their budget, and discovered they were $4,000 short per month with just under $100,000 of consumer debt. If those stressors weren't enough, Luke and Dianne had nine kids. (Yes, you read that right. That's three more than the

Brady Bunch!) These two were willing to do whatever it took to get out of debt fast.

Thankfully, Luke had a job where he had unlimited overtime opportunities. Yes, he was away from home a lot during their journey through the Pyramid, but the short-term sacrifice for the family's financial well-being allowed him to be present in the long run, without bills and debt collectors clouding his mind. Dianne helped out too, working extra hours to share the burden. In six months, they paid off $10,000 of debt. They had gotten out of the red and had a whopping $500–$1,000 extra set aside for debt every month. Two years later, they shared the following with me on social media that blew me away:

Every Friday (or sometimes Saturday) my husband gets up early and balances our budget. This isn't something we've always done. Heck, for a good chunk of our twenty years together, we let our bank account go negative. We borrowed money we couldn't pay back, and we even let our house go into foreclosure.

Thankfully, those are distant memories and two years ago we reached out to Justin Bennett. Our biggest hurdle was racked-up debt that had us living paycheck to paycheck. Luke and I both felt pretty hopeless financially when we had our first meeting with Justin. We had no idea how we could get ahead while barely staying afloat.

I am glad we put our trust in Justin's plan! Today we have more money than we've ever had . . . even though it's the same money we've always had! We have paid off over $70,000 in debt. We have our money working for us, and in just one more year, we plan to finally be ahead in life! Last Christmas was the first Christmas we didn't go into debt spoiling our kids, because we had put away a little each week *planning* for it! If you stress about money, reach out to Justin! I promise it will change your life!

Now, I'm flattered she said "I" changed her life, but really it wasn't me. It may have been my presentation of the material and my focus on accountability, but it was their commitment to the proven principles of the Pyramid that got them where they are now. Their situation was dire, yet they still reached financial freedom.

WHAT DOES IT TAKE?

Why are these stories so important to hear? Because you can't have it all. You can't have the meaningful and expensive CrossFit hobby and get out of debt. If you could, you'd already be there. It might not be a trendy workout community you can't let go of, but buying designer clothes for yourself and your kids, worshiping Whole Foods and refusing to eat anything but organic food, or owning a luxurious car because you believe it's who you are. Or maybe you think because your habits aren't high-priced ones, it won't matter if you keep them. But if you're buying a new book (or three) every week, grabbing fast-food lunches while working, or refusing to give up Netflix, it all adds up. Whatever it is, in order for financial freedom to work, there needs to be sacrifice. Think of your financial situation as if it were a flat-lining ER patient. Without intervention, this patient won't last until morning. But throughout the Awareness and Knowledge Levels, your finances become stabilized and removed from intensive care. However, they're not healthy yet. They're lying exhausted in a hospital bed, alive, but definitely not thriving. We've got to nurse your financial situation all the way back to health, which will require intervention (a.k.a. commitment).

While simply cutting a fifteen dollar subscription or saving a dollar on off-brand ketchup alone won't get you past surviving into thriving—it's radical changes that will—they shouldn't be discounted. Together they'll get you to your goals. Think what it would be like to have an extra $800 a month added to your income, or $500 less a month in bills to pay. What could that do for you?

Commitment did wonders for the people in these stories. They found more margin in their budgets and clear direction for their goals when they persevered through their "hard" and chose to be accountable. Are you willing to do what it takes to cross that finish line and take your money situation from dying, to stable, to thriving with your new habits and intentional plan?

CHOOSE YOUR HARD

Go back and review your short- and long-term goals from Chapter 2. Review the reasons why you want each one, then ask yourself if you're willing to stick with the hard now, so that more rewards than you could ever imagine can be yours later. Since you're inching closer to the top of the Pyramid, these goals are finally close enough to touch. You just need to commit.

So, ask your accountability partner or financial coach (you'll learn how to choose the right one in Chapter 9) to challenge you to move through the Pyramid by changing your habits and your mindset. There will be a point soon where you'll live like you never were in debt and like you made all the right choices the first time around. Finally, your money will be working for you, your family, and your dreams. Are you ready?

Chapter 7 Takeaways

- **Don't let up.** The faster you work through the early levels of the Financial Freedom Pyramid, the more quickly you'll launch into that idyllic period of life where you don't owe any money and your bank account is stocked with emergency cash.

- **After creating your first budget, you will discover one of three possibilities.** (1) It's balanced, but you still wonder, "Where did all my money go?" (2) It's not as bad as you thought. (3) It's worse than you thought.

- **The Commitment Level requires perseverance, accountability, and sacrifice.** Knowing what needs to change is good, but you have to pursue that change at all costs. More margin, clear direction, and a guiding hand can work miracles in your financial life. It's time to have a heart-to-heart with yourself.

- **You can't have it all.** Too many non-negotiables will make it impossible for you to reach your goals. You have to make real sacrifices in order to break the Cycle of Regret to reach financial freedom.

- **Choose your hard.** Cutting your lifestyle down to a bare minimum, starting a side hustle, and/or selling your car, etc., are the most common ways to accelerate you to the top of the Pyramid.

CHAPTER 8

Break the Cycle

The seed of every habit is a single, tiny decision.

—*James Clear,*
Atomic Habits

A COUPLE APPROACHED ME as everyone was leaving one of the first financial classes I taught. "We want to let you know," they said, "we've been through a class like this before and have read books on getting our finances under control, but we've always had one foot in and one foot out. We really weren't committed ... but we want to let you know before we really get going that we are all in." They understood the first two levels of the Pyramid but had never crossed over onto the Commitment Level.

"Great!" I said with enthusiasm and curiosity to see how they'd do. Every week the class participants would learn a new topic related to personal finance. As a part of our time together, each person would share what was working and what wasn't as they trekked through the Baby Steps and the Pyramid. For this couple, it seemed like every week they were focused on and executing all their next steps with ease. I was excited for them to finally cross this important milestone of commitment that was sure to propel them through the Momentum Level and onto freedom.

About halfway through the class, they hit a bump in the road. No problem. Hurdles happen to everyone at the Commitment Level. I was eager to hear their response to the struggle so the rest of the class could be inspired by their commitment. I was not expecting to be inspired myself. The wife said, "I just found out my dad has terminal cancer and has two months to live. So now every chance I get I am going home to see my dad who lives in another state. The extra money that was going to debt is now going to extra food, extra fuel, hotel stays, etc. If we were not all in on managing our finances the right way, we would be putting everything on a credit card."

As sad as that is to lose a parent, you could tell the woman had a sense of peace. She could focus 100 percent on her dad and not worry about money for the first time in her adult life. This is the power of commitment! It comes with *real* comfort and *real* freedom. Not the kind you get from splurging on new shoes or leasing a new car.

Interestingly, two weeks later I shared this story with a client named Matt. After a short pause, he said, "You know what's sad? When my mom passed away a few years ago, we were in that woman's same position except we *did* put all those extra expenses on credit cards. To this day, we're still paying off those expenses we charged to our credit cards. Every month, that payment is a painful reminder of two sad realities—the death and the debt."

THE CYCLE OF REGRET

The Cycle of Regret is sneaky. You don't realize you're rationalizing, changing your standards, or just giving up. But once you see it, you can feel hopeless to correct your mistakes, and you keep going with them. Often, we sit with our complacent attitude until something financially devastating happens. It's a wake-up call that either lifts us up and pushes us on to get out of the mess, or it drives us back down, providing the perfect excuse to quit, run, and wallow. Does this sound like you? We've all been there in some way.

Whether it's with finances, dieting, working out, or putting together that 8,000-piece Lego Millennium Falcon. Even if you are serious about commitment, it's still hard to stick with a plan and easy to fall into that same old cycle of wishing, rationalizing, rejecting, and despairing.

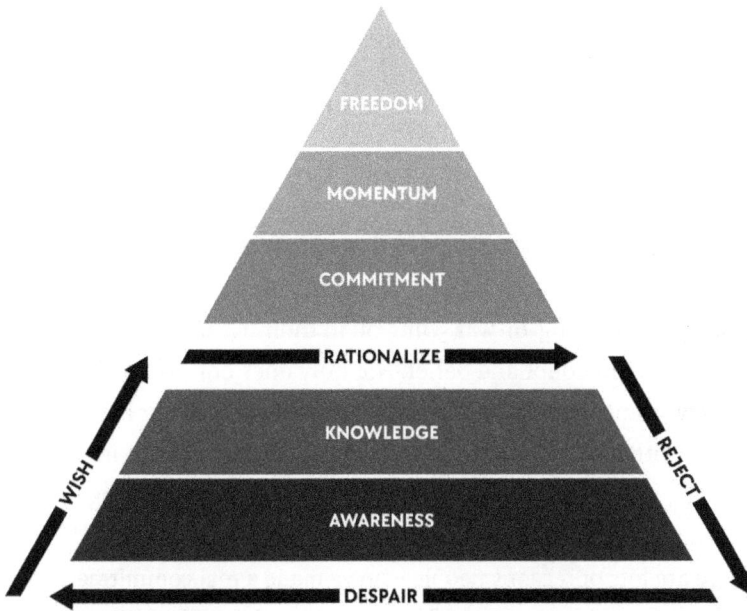

CYCLE OF REGRET

I often see this in my clients who are worn down, and the finish line feels more like a fantasy they hope will come true but doubt ever will, like when you blow out birthday candles, toss a coin in a fountain, or wish on a shooting star. Commitment to wishes doesn't amount to much. You didn't actually believe your wish to beat the final level of Pac-Man in front of your school crush would come true, and you don't actually believe your wish of reaching financial freedom will come true. When all you have is a wish, doubt is inevitable.

What we need to do is find a way to turn that wish into hope. That's one of the keys to pushing through the Commitment Level without returning to the Cycle of Regret. Author John C. Maxwell has a great quote that reads: "If you're committed, a failure doesn't mean that you'll never succeed. It just means you will take longer. Commitment makes you capable of failing forward until you reach your goals."[1] Avoiding the Cycle of Regret doesn't mean you won't have setbacks. It means that you believe so much in your hope-filled future, that even when things go south, you know to keep on going. But how do you go from wish to hope?

THE TUG OF WAR

There's no tool or fantasy program that's going to get you there. It's a mindset shift that doesn't happen overnight, and usually people feel an exhausting game of tug-of-war going on in their lives, feeling tossed back and forth between doubt and belief. Not only does our own will to find an "easier way" come into play, but so many other aspects of our lifestyle creep in to fill us with fear and defeat—transforming our strong hope in the future to a measly wish on a star for a better future. And like a shooting star, that wish quickly fades to despair.

There are lots of reasons people who've made a real commitment at the Commitment Level lose hope and fall back into the Cycle of Regret. Think of it like a New Year's resolution. You've probably set one of the top three New Year's resolutions for yourself at some point: lose weight, quit smoking, and get out of debt. If you're like most of the population, when you set your goals and commit to them at the beginning of the year, you're on fire and can clearly see that "future you" who doesn't smoke, overeat, or have any debt.

However, what always happens? Three weeks later you're eating a Twinkie, smoking a cigarette, and making payments on both purchases via your credit card. (Fun fact: One time I mixed this up on stage and told the crowd they were "smoking a Twinkie." Everyone thought it was pretty funny, except one man in the front row who said he'd tried it once and didn't recommend it.) Before you can reach your resolution, you need more than behavior change. You need to do more than stop smoking your

Twinkies for a few days, you need a complete mindset change. In order to have a mindset change, you need an environment change too. If you want to make changes in your finances, not only do you need to change what you do with your money, but you also need to be willing to change what's holding you back from staying hopeful and reaching financial freedom.

Negative influences are a big reason people get lost in the Cycle of Regret. If you have people in your social circle who are not committed to the same principles, process, and plan as you are, they're going to push against your radical, new way of life. It's true. You'll make people around you uncomfortable when you make big changes in your life.[2] If all your friends are smoking Twinkies, it's going to be hard to put yours down. Honestly, if people are pushing back on your plan, you should see this as a good sign, considering the state of American finances. However, I understand it can be difficult when everyone in your ear is saying you're doing the wrong thing. It can plant seeds of doubt, especially if they're close friends or family members.

The changes to your social life can be drastic if you're going all-in on your financial goals. It may mean no more weekly trips to the movie theater, no more evenings at the bar, no more joy rides in the dream car, no more monthly shopping trips with the girls, and no more extravagant vacations to post on Instagram. Not only is the loss of these things scary to face by themselves, but what about the social impact? Will your relationships with these friends fade away? Will they still invite you to the cookouts and birthday parties? Will they be offended you're not participating in the same lifestyle they are anymore? Will they think you're dumb or weird? These are real fears—especially if you're over twenty-five. Making friends is harder since your playground days and college years. However, even if you love these people, their negative habits could drag you back into your own. This is particularly true on the first three levels of the Pyramid when you haven't made much progress numbers-wise with your debt and savings totals.

Once you hit that Momentum Level, you may see big enough results to be unaffected by your friends' financially questionable shenanigans. But in order to avoid the Cycle of Regret, engaging with a new social group might better support and encourage your new money habits. Your mindset can more easily change with positive reinforcement. And new friends can take away some of the fear of losing the old ones. Let's be honest, if they're real friends, they'll still be there even if you're not golfing with them every weekend or bonding over boutique baby clothes.

I recommend finding some people locally or online that are going through the Financial Freedom Pyramid or following the same financial principles as you are. There are thousands who have gone through this plan, and they'll have plenty of wisdom to encourage you every step of the way. Their success will help you keep your hope from becoming a fleeting wish. A financial coach can also help change your mindset, and give you an accurate perspective of your situation and the foolproof principles you need to reach your goals. Doubt won't send you into the Cycle when you have a team pushing you forward. That's the power of accountability!

But there's another thing that often skews the mindset of people working through big goals like getting out of debt or quitting smoking. It's a failure to count the cost of their inaction. If you truly don't feel like what you're doing is harmful or urgent, it's incredibly easy to make excuses, doubt the possibility of success, and push the goal off for another time—or drop it altogether. Think of it this way: How many people in the 1960s thought about quitting smoking when no health risks were advertised? Probably very few.

What does that mean for you? Well, if you've got tremendous social support, and you still fall into the Cycle of Regret, it may be because you've never sat down with your notebook, pen, and calculator, and totaled up the true cost of your inaction, the true cost of putting off your debt-free journey for another time. In Chapter 1, we turned on the lights to understand the problems with your budget and spending habits. Similarly, we need to turn on the lights and discover how much your financial mistakes are costing you every year.

Credit card interest, not investing in retirement, putting nothing in savings every month, and letting your student loans sit there until you win the lottery are all scary ways your current habits are killing your future. Not literally like lung cancer would, but poor money habits are very real . . . and very scary. If you total up all expenses, the numbers are crazy! You're missing out on so much more than a few hundred or even thousand dollars. If we just look at your 401(k), or lack thereof, and consider the compound interest you could be earning (but aren't because your money is spent on debt payments), you're potentially missing out on *millions* of dollars, not thousands.

The median household income is $75,000.[3] Did you know if you're near this average, you will have had one million dollars pass through your hands in fourteen years? And if you only make $40,000 a year, you'll still have the same experience after twenty-five years. I share this to show you the power your income could have if you prioritize the right things and stay committed. Either of these incomes could translate to millions in retirement, thousands in savings, and a life of financial freedom if you stay committed. A financial coach can also help remind you of the reality of your inaction and shape your money mindset, so you can power through the Commitment Level, despite the hardships and setbacks.

I'm reminded of a client who told me over the phone the usual scenario: She and her husband lived paycheck to paycheck, had little savings, and were drowning in debt. Like everyone that calls, I was excited to work with her. However, a couple of weeks came and went, and I never heard back, which surprised me because at the end of the meeting she and her husband seemed excited. I followed up a couple of times, and when I finally got her on the phone, she told me she appreciated my time and knew she needed to do something, but this wasn't the right time. She'd call me back after school started.

Now, that was interesting. When she first contacted me, clearly, she and her husband wanted to get something done, but suddenly now was a bad time? I told her, "I have no problem calling you after school starts this fall, but can I tell you what will happen? I'll call you and you are going to say how busy you are. Then, you're going to explain how hard it is to get the family together for a meal, let alone together to meet with a coach. Then, you'll ask me to call you after the first of the year once Christmas is over. That way, you can start the new year fresh.

"Then I'll call you first thing next year," I continued, "and you'll tell me you overspent on Christmas and need to clean up some of your credit card debt, so I should call you after your tax refund comes in, about the time the kids get out of school.

"When the kids get out of school, I'll follow up with you, and you'll say that now is not a good time as the kids have summer camp, and we're taking a much needed family vacation. Could you call me when the kids are back in school? We'll finally be ready to work on our finances then."

I finished by sharing one of my favorite Zig Ziglar quotes, "If you wait until all the lights are green before you leave home, you'll never get started on your trip to the top."[4]

It was clear I'd taken her breath away. She paused and said, "Wow! It's like you know me! You're right, I'll probably keep finding a way to kick the can down the road." She needed to hear the truth, and after our talk, the couple were not only convinced to hire me as their coach, but to follow through with commitment.

The point is—don't put this off. Realize how much waiting for the right time is dragging you down and instead have a realistic outlook. The right time won't suddenly appear, especially when you're in debt and stressed about money. You must admit that what you're doing is harmful and needs to change for the benefit of your family's future. Action should be taken now and not delayed until the next New Year's resolution or big tax refund. It's time to stop smoking those Twinkies, and realize a better life is waiting for you at the top of the Pyramid.

GET ACTIVE

Think back to the goals you set at the start of your journey. Ask yourself if you really want those goals, and your answer would definitely be yes. Everyone wants their dream life. However, it's not really a question of if you want it . . . but if you want to *work* for it.

What if I told you I'd give you a million dollars in twelve months. Obviously, you'd gladly take the money. However, what if I said you had to stick to your budget verbatim for that whole twelve months. Would you really want to work for it? I bet you would. It's not a matter if you *can* do it, it's a matter if you *will* do it. The reward at the end of the finish line would be so sweet. This is how you should see your journey through the Pyramid.

You need both the motivating end reward and the present commitment to do what it takes. It's time to get to work!

Getting active is the best way to combat the Cycle of Regret. The world tells us if we don't feel energized or disciplined to take on our goals, we have to go hunting and soul-searching to find the motivation *before* we get started. The reality is action comes first, *then* motivation. The Bible alludes to this in Proverbs 13:12 when it says, "Hope deferred makes the heart sick, but a desire fulfilled is a tree of life" (ESV). The tangible and emotional rewards of the accomplished task make you totally energized and ready to take on more.

There was a day not so long ago when I came home from the office completely worn out, and I knew there was another long day ahead. After I ate my dinner, I started up the stairs, ready to sink into my bed for the night. Before I covered three or four stairs, my wife kindly asked me to put my dirty dishes into the dishwasher.

I had to stifle a groan because it was the last thing I wanted to do. However, I love my wife and understood she had a long day too, so after grumbling a little, I went back down the stairs and started loading the dishwasher. To be honest, I was annoyed, but as I carried on with the chore, I suddenly found myself more awake and charged to do the task. Soon, I not only loaded my dishes into the dishwasher, but all the dirty dishes into the dishwasher! Seeing the clean counter was so satisfying and knowing that I was making my wife happy made it even better. When I finished the chore, I asked her if there was any other task I could take off her list before I went to bed. Did you catch that? I had a big change of heart . . . *after* I saw the fruit of my actions.

The point is you may not feel like doing the work to get your finances in order. Budgeting, cutting out extra expenses, getting a second job, and zeroing in on your poor money habits may not be something that excites you, but once you get that first victory, a stream of hope will flow from a slow-moving current to a cascading waterfall and your motivation will follow. You'll be like a runner afraid of that first hurdle, but as you get in a rhythm of clearing every obstacle, you experience more and more energy to push through to the end. By the fourth or fifth hurdle, you won't even fear the sixth. You'll have confidence to overcome it. Soon, that finish line will be in sight and that's when you'll run the fastest.

HOPE DRIVES MOTIVATION

Whether it's getting your emergency fund together or paying off a family loan, your victories will lead to more victories. So, if you're not feeling the motivation right now, stick with me as your coach, and we'll find it together one win at a time. Remember the process: First comes action, then comes motivation . . . then comes hope. Don't wait for the right moment. If you're waiting for the right time to get your finances together, you'll simply never get started.

And if you don't commit to a plan right now (yes, right now) your money situation will continue to worsen. Without your action, there's no magic moment where things just "work themselves out." You're either moving toward financial freedom or away from it. There is no in-between. Please don't bank on a lottery win, inheritance from a distant relative, or a return on investment from your 1990s Beanie Baby collection. Even when you fall down, as long as you're committed, you're not moving away from financial freedom, you're "failing forward" into your goals. Think about the runner, even if they knock over the hurdle, they're still closer to the finish line. You're getting closer too. You might be tripping and stumbling along now, but before long, you'll catch your stride and you'll have no doubt you'll finish the race!

Chapter 8 Takeaways

- **Avoiding the Cycle of Regret doesn't mean you won't have setbacks.** When you fall down, as long as you're committed, you're not moving away from financial freedom, you're "failing forward" into your goals.

- **An accountability partner or financial coach helps change your mindset.** Doubt won't send you into the Cycle of Regret when you have a team giving you an accurate perspective of your situation and pushing you forward to reach your goals.

- **Count the cost of inaction.** You must admit that what you're doing is harmful and needs to change for the benefit of your family's future.

- **No more excuses.** Pushing down the road what you need to do now won't accomplish anything. It's time to get to work!

- **Combat the Cycle of Regret with action.** Your victories will lead to more victories. Remember, first comes action, then comes motivation . . . then comes hope. Don't wait for the right moment. If you're waiting for the right time to get your finances together, you'll simply never get started.

CHAPTER 9

The Accountability Gap

Tactical commitments are not enough. If there is no relational commitment anywhere, then there's no accountability.

—Sam Silverstein,
The Theory of Accountability

I'D LOVE TO TELL YOU once you've committed to a plan and have begun to experience hope, that you've unlocked all the key ingredients for a successful journey toward your goals. But the truth is there will still be setbacks. No matter how much I've prepared you for the hard times . . . they're still hard! The temptation to give up and accept your always broke reality is tremendous, especially if circumstances are asking you to give up more than you think is possible. Maybe you can't reach financial freedom with two jobs and have to get a third. Maybe you thought you could pull this off *and* keep your kids in all their activities, but there isn't any margin. Maybe you really thought keeping the newer car was doable, but that high car payment is eating up too much of your income before you can use it for your goals. These things are *hard*. It's easy to give up on your commitment at this stage because you feel so paralyzed by your day-to-day decisions and you stop taking action, which causes you to lose motivation, and finally, drop your commitment and stumble back into the Cycle.

This situation describes the disconnect that prevents people from going from Knowledge to Commitment. There's a gap between what you want to do and what you can do. You might have the skills and talent, but not the mental fortitude to overcome the drama of big setbacks, overwhelming temptations, and devastating circumstances. The feelings can get so intense that stopping the present negative emotions becomes more important to you than reaching your goals. You just want to stop the *hard*. Despite being committed to your plan, there's still a missing piece you need to get you through the hard—accountability. Accountability is the essential component to your new personal finance habits that'll take you from failure to freedom.

And when I say essential, I mean it. No matter who you are, you need some level of accountability. For some, accountability may be a monthly meeting with friends. For others, accountability may be a regular check-in with a paid coach. It depends on how much you struggle to go from Knowledge to Commitment. If you've tried before and failed to get your finances in order, you need to face it—accountability is essential. There's no reason to be ashamed of that either. Accountability helps us in so many ways every day, whether it's driving the speed limit because of the accountability of law enforcement or trying your best at work because of the accountability of your manager. Accountability helps us be our best and perform at our peak. It's time to stop pretending you can do all this alone. To feel motivation and power through the hardships, you need an accountability partner.

ARE YOU ALL IN?

As a financial coach, I am that accountability partner. I can think of many instances when my clients wanted to forget about their goals and go back to their false comfort, but that would have landed them right back into the Cycle of Regret. Having an accountability partner (a coach, in this case), saved them from that disaster.

I could give you plenty of examples, but the one that sticks out most was the story of a couple named Greg and Lisa. They had been with me for six months and were making great progress. They had paid off a good amount of debt, were sticking to the budget, and were picking up momentum every month as they pushed toward their financial goals. However, in our January meeting, I could tell right away something was off. I could see it in their faces, so I said, "Uh-oh... I don't think I am going to like what I'm about to hear."

Lisa blurted, "I'm going to tell you right now we overspent at Christmas... and not just a little bit. We overspent a lot. We used a credit card, and we're okay with it. Our children deserve to have a nice Christmas."

I'm thinking, *Okay, that was a bad call, but we can get past this.* Just as I was about to give my reply, Lisa interrupted me and continued, "Oh, and by the way, my husband and I made the decision we deserve a nice vacation since we work so hard, and our daughters are going to be off on their own soon. We booked an all-inclusive trip to Cancun." At this point, I was incredulous and asked, "How are you going to pay for the trip?"

"With the credit card," she stated almost proudly. Again, as I was about to give my response, Greg butted in, "And I've decided not to sell my truck to pay off debt. Instead, I am looking to upgrade to something better." As they went on talking, trying to convince me that these were good ideas, I pulled up my notes on screen from their first session. When it popped up, it was now Greg's turn to say, "Uh-oh!"

At the beginning of the first session, I always ask clients how far they want to be pushed to reach their goals on a scale of 1–10. Greg and Lisa gave me a ten, probably because they knew they'd struggle with sticking with good money habits. They got tight-lipped seeing their earlier answer. I reminded them why they hired me as a coach and reminded them they'd taken the same financial class twice and hit the Cycle of Regret both times at this same juncture. They really needed discipline, a changed mindset, and reminders of the cost of their money mistakes to stick with their plan.

I told them there's a narrow path to financial freedom, and if they didn't stop rationalizing their habits, they would soon be rejecting their financial plan, and no matter how much money they made or how much they paid me, they'd never reach the Freedom Level. I finished by telling them they needed to go on a date (budgeted first) and discuss if they were all in, or if they were out.

When I met with them again, they told me they had made the decision to continue forward thanks to the accountability I provided for them. I was happy to hear that and could see genuine regret on their faces for the decisions they made during Christmas that were irreversible. In between sessions, they'd taken their Cancun vacation, so I asked how it went. Greg said they had a wonderful time and described some of the things they did in detail, while Lisa sat there silently with her arms folded and her eyes downcast. When Greg finished, I asked Lisa, "What did you think of the vacation?"

She acknowledged me but continued looking down as she searched for her answer. Before she could speak, I said, "You didn't enjoy this trip very much, did you?"

"No, I didn't!" she finally looked up and explained.

"Was there another adult on this trip you didn't mean to bring along?" I asked with a smirk. She saw where I was going and with a humorous smile, she shouted, "Yes, you!"

"Too bad I didn't get to enjoy all those excursions Greg was talking about." We all laughed and it broke the tension.

"I could not get you out of my head the entire trip," Lisa shared. "I knew you were right. We had no business being on a trip like that, and I knew we needed to get home and stay focused on the plan. I just wanted to go to the customer service desk and ask them to take it all back!"

Lisa was filled with regret her whole trip, and now they were restarting the Pyramid. They had created significant setbacks for themselves, but fortunately weren't at ground zero. Once again, they decided they were all in, but knew they needed my accountability to keep them on track. Without it, they'd continue to rationalize and decide they deserved more than what their financial plan allowed. I'm happy to report they learned from their mistakes and reached the Freedom Level in just a few years. They paid off all their debt, their savings is fully funded, and they're building a home on an acreage where they can live out the future they've dreamed of. They were where you are now. They made it, and so can you.

EVERYONE NEEDS A COACH

Greg and Lisa were able to do what they did because of their own hard work, but without accountability to remind them to stay the course, they would have never made it. Like many others, the temptation to quit took hold of them dozens of times throughout their journey, and they needed another voice to chime in and create hope while reminding them of the future they'd lose if they gave up. It's a powerful thing to have an accountability partner available to identify your struggle and push you through it to refuel you and inspire you.

As I mentioned earlier, it can feel embarrassing to need someone to help you accomplish something. It might make you feel stupid, undisciplined, immature, irresponsible, and that shame may keep you from establishing accountability and securing your future goals. But there's no reason to feel shame. Needing accountability doesn't say anything negative about who you are and what you're capable of. We could all use a coach, for one thing or another.

The truth is, the average person is only disciplined in one or two areas, and these areas are usually not money and fitness. Take my wife and I for example. We are both very disciplined with our money, and accountability isn't necessary for us to achieve our goals. However, diet and exercise? That's another story! Without the accountability of a coach, I can't make progress past the Commitment Level, and neither can my wife. We don't have the mental stamina to push through temptation and stay disciplined when it comes to our physical health. So Jessica and I hired a coach and got to work. In a year, we dropped weight, felt healthier, and established much better habits. (It was cool being on the other end of the coaching experience too!)

As the year closed, we proved we had the ability to maintain our habits on our own, so we decided to graduate ourselves from coaching. We both did well the first few months: We didn't overeat, we continued to workout, and we didn't gain back any of the weight. Amazing! Jessica was particularly excited because she had struggled for years to lose the weight she gained during the pregnancies of our five kids. Over the years, she had bought several books and online classes in an attempt to accomplish her goals, but each would simply give her awareness of the root problems and knowledge of the pathway to successful weight loss. No matter which approach she tried, she always started with a sense of enthusiasm and hope, and after getting the awareness and knowledge she was looking for, she would commit to their process. However, you know how this story goes: cue the Cycle of Regret. In fact, it got to the point where I would get frustrated because with each new system she found, she would say something like, "This is it! This is why all of those haven't worked in the past." I got sick of hearing it.

Despite the excitement at finding her "ticket to freedom," Jessica would hit a wall, lose hope, and eventually decide the program she thought was her key to happiness wasn't for her after all. Despair and disappointment would lead her back to overeating and avoiding exercise. Our critical inner voice says, "Come on! Just stick with it!" But we all know that's much easier said than done, whether you're working towards a financial goal or a fitness goal.

So what changed for Jessica? The coach! Our coach provided the accountability she desperately needed to stick to her commitment, even when the going got tough. I remember during one of our coaching sessions,

Jessica was crying because she'd hit another wall and was tired of fighting the same battle over and over. She felt like her goals would never come to fruition, and she should accept her current stalled situation.

That was a tough time in her fitness journey, but our coach was able to seize the moment and encourage Jessica to continue. She lacked hope, but our coach reminded her of the progress she'd already made and provided some expert advice. Jessica agreed to continue, even when she felt like it was pointless. It was a few weeks later that Jessica was crying tears of joy because she got past the wall that blocked her and had regained hope for the future. After that, nothing could stop her momentum! Jessica stuck to the program even after we graduated from coaching and continued to see progress. Of course, there were times she faltered, but because of the tools our coach gave us, she was always able to reset, refocus, and charge her way forward again.

Though Jessica saw huge success after coaching ... the same was not true for me. I also had big health goals I wasn't able to accomplish on my own. I brought plenty of bad habits and daily struggles to my coach hoping to see the same progress. While in coaching, I did great. I was eating well, I found a great workout routine, and I saw big results in my health and weight.

But a few months after coaching ended? I totally abandoned everything I'd committed to. I was back to eating those triple cheeseburgers and not working out. A year after fitness coaching, I stepped on the scale and realized I weighed more than I ever had. To say I was ashamed would be an understatement. I was definitely in the "despair" state of the Cycle of Regret.

However, I finally got to that fork-in-the-road moment where I knew I had to choose a path: Continue the DIY approach to losing weight or reach my goals by getting accountability. There was no third option. While I was deciding what to do, the small group I was a part of in our church decided to hold each other accountable to whatever goals we wanted to reach. This was exactly what I needed for my health goals! Accountability is essential for me, and I did still need someone (or lots of someones!) in my corner, keeping me on track. This may be cause for embarrassment for some people, but I know everyone needs accountability in some area of life. For you, it's finance. For me, it's fitness.

In my group, I shared that I wanted to lose twenty-six pounds that year and demonstrate I could be disciplined and God-honoring in this area. Next thing I knew, the group helped me break down my journey into three-pound increments, and each accountability partner took a different checkpoint and committed to holding me accountable to it. This was *super* motivating. Especially considering one of our group members was ex-military and said if I went backward, he'd knock at my door at 4:00 a.m. with a radio blaring outside while I did push-ups on the lawn till I puked. Talk about motivation!

The group was exactly the supercharged accountability system I needed to reach my goals. In the first month, I lost twelve pounds. That was almost half of my goal accomplished—in one month. I kept going, and though the next few pounds didn't shed quite as quickly, my group didn't lose hope. They reminded me of what I'd already accomplished, and I continued. After six months I'd reached my goal. Normally, I would have stopped there with the accountability group, but I'd lost this weight once before, putting it all back on the moment the accountability stopped. So, for the rest of the year, our church group kept me accountable to keep the weight off, to continue exercising, and to maintain good eating habits. Though I do that now, I still check in with my group regularly about my health because this is an area I struggle in. With accountability, my shortcoming in fitness won't hold me back from living well and respecting the body God gave me. With accountability, I always have hope and direction.

This is why accountability is so important for your finances. Like my wife and I, you've probably tried countless times to lose weight, pay off debt, or build savings and failed. I honestly believe the other programs Jessica enthusiastically showed me would have worked, but without commitment and accountability, a well-researched plan can only get you so far.

In the Financial Freedom Pyramid Guide, I told you how everyone needs a coach, whether for one time or for a lifetime. Maybe you need a coach long enough to get past the first couple of hurdles and then, like my wife, you can do it on your own. Or, maybe you're like me and need coaching and accountability for a lifetime. At the end of the day, winners hire a coach. If a person has proven they can't get the results they want from self-discipline, accountability is the key. Accountability is the thing that'll bridge the gap between failure and freedom.

ACCOUNTABILITY GIVES YOU STRENGTH

Studies show that once people have identified their finish line, they're 10 percent more likely to complete the goal.[1] However, once you commit to the goal and consciously make the decision to move forward with it, you're 25 percent more likely to achieve it. Then, making a plan for when and how you'll do it increases your chances of reaching your goal, the Freedom Level, to 50 percent. Here we go! That's the Commitment Level.

Okay, what does this have to do with accountability? The study didn't stop there. It found that sharing your plan with someone will move you to a 65 percent chance of completing your goal. But where the numbers get really crazy is when you add in a specific accountability appointment with a partner or coach. Your chances of success go from 65 percent all the way to 95 percent.

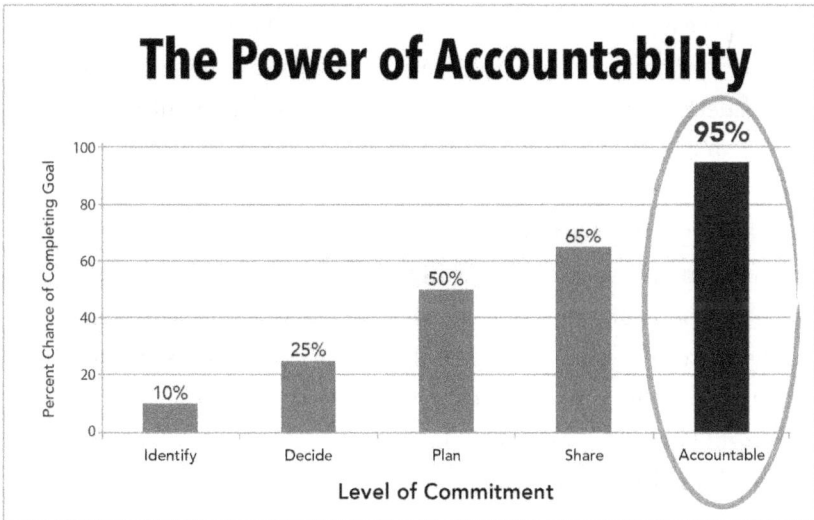

The Power of Accountability

Wow! When you commit to the plan and commit with an accountability partner, you've squashed the possibility of the Cycle of Regret, taking out your final adversary before it can derail true financial freedom. At the Commitment Level, you'll start to see a debt paid off here and there. You'll likely see your income increase. Your bank account and budget will often be under control and working for your goals. Confirmation that this plan works is incredibly freeing and hopeful.

Accountability is the missing piece. In your "I've tried it all" history with financial plans, you've probably never tried this. When choosing your accountability partner, ensure they hold these five characteristics to push you to your goals:

1. Share your vision

If your accountability partner does not line up with the sound financial principles you've learned so far, the advice they give you won't align with your vision for financial freedom. You need someone who is going to talk you *out* of debt, not try to get you to open more credit cards or lease a car.

2. Trustworthy

For an accountability partner to be effective, you have to trust them and be willing to be honest and open with them. No secrets! They can't help you if you're not vulnerable. If you won't tell them when you mess up or when you make a decision outside of your principles, there's no point in having an accountability partner.

3. Ask tough questions

You need to give your accountability partner the green light to ask you tough questions, and they need to be willing to ask them. Whether they're asking you to give something up for the sake of your goals, or they're asking you to explain why you went back on your principles, they've got to ask, and you've got to answer. This will help you both get to the root of your issues and quickly move out of deep ruts.

4. Firm, but kind

Over the years, I have seen some accountability partners use this respon-sibility as an opportunity to be a jerk. Unless you specifically ask for someone to be up in your face and make you give them ten push-ups for each dollar you overspend, then a drill-sergeant-style accountability partner won't be helpful. What you're looking for is someone that can give discerning feedback but also be lovingly firm when they need to be.

5. Tell you no

A big benefit to hiring a coach is they're not your friend or family member first. When someone has a personal relationship with you, it'll be harder for them to tell you no. If they're your shopping buddy and always tell you you "deserve" an impulse buy, you won't see results. No has to be your accountability partner's favorite word.

THERE'S POWER IN ACCOUNTABILITY—NOT SHAME

I hope you can see there's so much power in accountability. When you have others on your side to drive you forward, reaching goals no longer feels impossible. Proverbs 27:17 says, "Iron sharpens iron, and one man sharpens another." Your accountability partner, coach, or group won't let you falter, because they care about you. They care about you so much, they'll push you on even when you don't care anymore. An accountability partner will pick you back up every time you fall and keep you moving forward. You'll be committed not only to the process, but to them. Not letting them down or wasting their time adds to the fire that fuels you to continue forward.

My client Amber needed an accountability partner because she was managing her household as a single parent. She was a natural spender, so part of our coaching plan was she'd call me any time she was about to spend money outside of the budget. Not long after our first session, she called me and said, "Justin, I've had a bad day at work, and I'm going shopping." (Sounds like some of those bad habits and false comfort, huh?) She continued, "You'll be proud of me, though. I'll get something we need. The kids need school clothes for next month."

"How much do you have saved to buy clothes?" I asked.

"Forty bucks."

"Where do you plan on shopping?"

"The mall," she said without hesitation.

She had done a good job budgeting that forty dollars the previous month like we set out. However, I knew forty dollars wasn't going to get her far at the mall, and she'd probably be tempted to overspend. I told her shopping was okay, but I added a caveat. "Instead of going to the mall," I said, "I'd like you to go to a thrift store like Goodwill." I had barely finished before she raised her voice in frustration and gave me a few words you wouldn't hear in church. She hung up before I could respond.

"Wow," I said and went on with my day. People don't usually swear at me, but it's not unusual as an accountability partner to receive pushback. That's what having a partner is all about. To push back when you push back! Amber called me back two hours later. When I saw her name pop up, I took a deep breath. But when I answered, she had a totally different demeanor. She exclaimed, "Justin! I am so excited. I had to call you. I just left Goodwill and I was able to buy all my kids school clothes. I literally have bags of clothes on both of my arms and I was able to stay within my forty-dollar budget. I'm so sorry I yelled at you and hung up. Thank you for being there in my weak moment."

Do you see the power? If Amber was on her own after work that day, she would have gone to the mall and overspent. Then where would she be? Back in that Cycle of Regret. I can't express enough how important accountability is to your commitment. It's the key that'll unlock your true potential and give you the power you need to go from the Awareness Level all the way to the Freedom Level. You just need to find your person, share your goals, and take action.

Do you have a mentor or someone you trust that has done well with money? Ask if they are willing to meet with you and hold you accountable to reaching your goals. Don't know of anyone that you can trust? Consider joining an online community where you can ask questions and learn what other people have done when they got stuck. This also gives you a place to celebrate your accomplishments along your journey to financial freedom. If none of these options apply, consider hiring a coach. No matter what or who you choose, I want to be a part of your accountability plan in some way. So, email me right now at justin@levelupyourfinances.com and in the subject line type, "STOP THE CYCLE." In the body of the email, share with me (1) what you'll do to achieve financial freedom and (2) that yes, you've picked an accountability partner to get you there, and I'll respond back to you. If you're committed to this process, I want to know about it. I want you to feel one more layer of accountability—one more person in your corner rooting for you and believing in your journey. Finally, the answer to why you haven't reached your goals is clear—you needed accountability. Someone else to help you get a better perspective on your financial life and encourage you to make the choices you deserve, the choices to finally win with your money.

Chapter 9 Takeaways

- **No shame in accountability.** Accountability helps us be our best and perform at our peak. You are 95 percent more likely to succeed if you're accountable to a third party.

- **Everyone needs a coach, whether for one time or for a lifetime.** Whether it's to get past the first couple of hurdles or all the way to the end, coaching and accountability are useful for a lifetime. At the end of the day, winners hire a coach.

- **An accountability partner with these five characteristics will push you toward your goal.** They share your vision, are trustworthy, ask tough questions, are firm but kind, and tell you no.

- **Find someone to hold you accountable.** Do you have a mentor or someone you trust that has done well with money? Ask if they are willing to hold you accountable to reaching your goals. Don't know of anyone that you can trust? Contact a professional financial coach.

- **Email me at justin@levelupyourfinances.com.** If you're committed to this process, I'll be one more layer of accountability, one more person in your corner rooting for you and believing in your journey.

CHAPTER 10

The Struggle to Commit

Nothing happens until you commit, and it's only after you commit that you know what freedom feels like.

—*Dan Sullivan,*
10X Is Easier Than 2X

MOST PEOPLE FINISH A GREAT BOOK or podcast on personal finance feeling inspired and motivated to take on whatever is ahead, excited to apply the new information and change their habits. Each time this happens, they are certain it'll work out, but you can tell me what happens next— you've been here before! After a few months, your drive is gone, your hope runs dry, and the head knowledge isn't enough to take you across the finish line. You give up, fall back into old habits, and end up back at the beginning of the race again. That's the Cycle of Regret. Each time you go around, that finish line feels less and less possible to reach.

If you're feeling excited and ready to apply my advice, great! But as your coach, I need to ask you: What will be different this time than all the other times before? Being excited and hopeful isn't enough, especially if you've been through the Cycle of Regret plenty of times. True commitment is essential for breaking free of these shackling cycles. This chapter is all about preparing you for when that lightbulb of discovery and enthusiasm burns out and things get tough. At some point in this process of going through the Pyramid, you'll reach your fork-in-the-road moment, where you have to decide if you're going to commit and carry on with the hard work or go back to the false comfort of your old ways.

This part is hard. *Really* hard. I know this is not what you want to hear, but trust me, this is the part you need to hear. Without commitment you *will* fail because hardships are coming no matter how solid the strategy is. However, if you plan for the challenges that come with the Commitment Level, you'll be equipped to tackle these hurdles, instead of throwing your hands up and saying something like

"This is great for people in the upper class, but not for people at my income level."

"There is nothing for me to sacrifice, so there's no way to make the plan work."

"The plan doesn't work for someone like me. My situation is unique."

"I'm just not good with money. I can't do it."

But you're getting to your goal with no excuses this time! I know you can do this. Everyone can follow these principles and overcome their situation with the right focus and willingness. It's no secret many people will take shortcuts and hope that somehow everything works itself out. They will see Betty, the eighty-one-year-old widow, who could never retire as a personal finance anomaly instead of the norm. Really, though, Betty's money situation *is* the norm, and that normal is terrifying. That's the future you can look forward to if you give up on the Commitment Level and return to the Cycle of Regret for a final time, choosing instead to live in a perpetual state of remorse.

I know that sounds intense, but I want you to see the obvious fork-in-the-road path and choose freedom over captivity. Choose joy over sorrow. Choose peace over stress. Choose victory over regret. I really hope you will make the right choice and stay committed all the way through, but I see three main things stopping clients from making the right choice.

1. Fear of giving up comforts
2. Fear of repeating past failures
3. Fear of making big sacrifices

Commitment is one of the hardest and scariest things anyone can do. In order to fully commit, you have to let go of something—either a fear of failure, the pain of an earlier experience, or something you really love. Let me give you the honest truth: If you're not willing to let go of whatever is holding you back and commit 100 percent to your future, you will fail. That pain from the past will linger, and eventually you'll lose your current lifestyle forever. (Remember, you don't want to be eighty-one working sixty hours a week!)

The reality of falling into a deeper financial hole is scary, but for many of us, changing our ways is even scarier. It's easy to continue on our path of poor financial discipline and stumble our way through paycheck-to-paycheck living for the rest of our lives. What takes real courage is committing to changing our habits and establishing a new way of life. I define courage as making a decision you don't want to make, while being uncomfortable, anxious, and possibly down-right scared. You know deep down that taking this courageous step is the right thing to do. But taking the first step is almost always the hardest, and the temptation to go down that old path will be there. But if you have the courage to commit and prepare for those weak moments, you can overcome anything, even these three common but crippling financial fears:

1. FEAR OF GIVING UP COMFORTS

Anything we do every day can be a comfort—even if it's bad for us. Swiping a credit card, refusing to look at your bank account, splurging at the grocery store, and ignoring your concerning financial future can all be simple things that are keeping you in the red, but also keeping you warm and cozy in your current financial mess.

It's a strange paradox, isn't it? The same thing that brings us a ton of stress and anxiety also helps make us feel safe in familiar territory. I see this all the time with clients and their credit cards. These massive monthly payments and high interest rates weigh them down every day. Not only do they owe a lot of money, but they also can't do much with their paychecks because it's all getting sucked away to creditors. It's exhausting and frustrating to have debt preventing you from going forward.

However, it feels nice to know there's something you can swipe if a big expense comes up (or there's a sale you just can't pass up.) You may find a lot of security in that credit card, but remember that credit limit is not a gift, it's a curse. You know those movies where the characters make some deal with an imaginary genie to get something they really want, but it ends up coming at a much greater cost than it was worth? That's credit cards! They make you feel for a second like you're getting what you want, until the realization comes crashing down that you weren't given anything. Something really important was taken from you—your freedom.

Unhealthy money comforts, like online shopping or fast-food lunches, might relieve your stressful day or fuel you through a long shift, but then what? Comfort quickly turns to confinement when your daily money habits lock you into that Cycle of Regret. It takes courage to break free from the comfort that leads to confinement. Author Mike Michalowicz calls this "the Survival Trap." An unhealthy situation that "When something is familiar, it becomes comfortable. And while you may say you 'hate it' and 'can't take it anymore,' the truth is, you are familiar with it ... and, when you are familiar with something, as ugly as it is, it is easier to keep doing it."[1]

Commitment implies a willingness to sacrifice comforts in order to reach a goal. If you've been trying to make a financial plan stick for a long time, you've probably made small cuts here and there like cutting subscriptions and gym memberships. However, for some of us, a bigger sacrifice (a.k.a. a bigger discomfort) is needed to save money, pay off debt, and finally move from commitment to momentum to freedom, the final level of the Pyramid. This could mean suspending retirement investments, selling the car you can't afford, moving somewhere cheaper, getting an extra job, and/or selling everything in your home. Yes, these are big things that take courage, but you can't let false comforts keep you from crossing that finish line.

2. FEAR OF REPEATING PAST FAILURES

There are a lot of ways you may have been burned in the past with finances—and those burns might still sting. I see clients come in all the time where early experiences with money shaped their thought processes, and they struggle to get out of that mindset. For some people, it's simply the fact that they've messed up a lot, and every intentional money step forward actually plunged them into a deeper hole. Maybe they took out a home equity line of credit (HELOC) for renovations and almost lost their home because of it. Maybe they leased a new car, and the high payments and restrictions sent their account into the red numerous times. Or maybe they took out student loans they can't pay, and are suffocating, watching the principal get higher and higher.

Since these choices are often seen as "good financial" moves in our culture, believing that the plan I've laid out will actually pay off any differently may seem far-fetched to you. You may have the mindset that the whole system is built against you and any personal-finance plan out there is a scam. This belief has you stuck in an attitude of, "I'm down, and I can never get back up. There is no help for me."

If you've ever been fooled by bad money advice, I feel for you, I really do. It takes a lot of courage to trust financial advice again if you've been wronged by bad tips for years. Remember, I made tons of stupid money mistakes based on what I thought was right. However, there is a correct way to do this thing, and it does work if you believe it. It's like Henry Ford said, "Whether you believe you can do a thing or not, you are right." You have to believe it can be different and let go of the guilt, shame, and anger from past money mistakes, or nothing changes.

I've also had clients locked into bad habits and poor perspectives from their parents. If my client's parents weren't smart with money and regularly preached principles contrary to the ones I've laid out, it can be really hard for people to reconcile that. Even if they see their parents still struggling with their finances, they may have a deep fear of missing out on the same lifestyle they had or a deep fear of somehow dishonoring their childhood by doing something different. If this is you, put those fears behind you and remember that your life is your own. You don't need to justify or judge the actions of your parents or anyone else.

Take some time to acknowledge the past, release it, and start again with a clean slate and spirit of courage. You don't need to get approval from your parents to change the way you handle money. You're getting your life back on track, and finally being free from the stress and anxiety you feel will be proof enough you made the right choice when the time comes. On that same note, you can't blame your parents for your bad habits either. These habits are now yours, regardless of where they came from. If you see they're toxic or unhelpful, it's time for you to commit to change and drop the blame game. The blame game never helped anyone get to the top of the Pyramid.

The last way I see the past holding people back is when money is tied up with another type of relationship—marriage. I meet lots of married couples where one spouse is not committed to working together on their finances, and the other spouse is left carrying the weight of it alone. Whether your past marriage was plagued with financial infidelity, financial abuse, or other types of financial trauma, or your current marriage is plagued with them, it can fill you with anxiety, fear, and dread to work on finances together when the past has only brought hurt to your marriage. If this is you, things will be painful at first, and all these emotions *will* come up. It might seem impossible to overcome the emotions that come with taking control of your money. But don't give up.

If your spouse hasn't been supportive in the past, let them know how tremendously helpful it would be if they would take responsibility for the finances alongside you. If they're willing, this would be a great time to bring in a financial coach to guide you in working together in this important area of your lives. If they're not willing, you may need to consult a marriage counselor or therapist to help you through the difficulty and get you started with your financial goals. Once you do, you'll begin to develop positive memories and associations with your money. I'm not saying it'll be easy, but don't go down the path of financial failure to avoid facing your past. It's time to find the courage to push through until you and your spouse are working together on your finances, and your past failures are irrelevant to your current success.

3. FEAR OF MAKING BIG SACRIFICES

I was working with a couple, Cody and Alexis, who had $177,000 in consumer debt. Their debt was from anything you could imagine: personal loans, credit cards, student loans, family loans, and more. At the time I met them, they had sold their home and were moving out of state. We discussed renting first and waiting to purchase a house until they got out of debt, which would only take a couple of years since the proceeds from the sale of their house would cover a significant chunk of what was owed. It was a great plan. As long as they were committed to it, they'd have this huge boost in their Pyramid journey that would give them the momentum to ride it out until they hit the Freedom Level. I was pumped for them!

However, at the next meeting, I couldn't have been less prepared for what I heard. The session started on a sour note. It was a video meeting, and after we shared the usual niceties, Alexis blurted, "You're going to kill us." She said it with a slight smile as she shook her head.

I was not so amused. With a raised brow, I thought cautiously, *How bad can it be?* Often when people insinuate they went off the plan, they're referring to going slightly over budget or putting an unexpected repair on a credit card. (Both are no-nos, but workable.) Since this was one of the early sessions, I wasn't too worried about it. It takes time to change your behavior and commit to your budget and financial plan.

Finally, she said, "We actually bought two cars and financed them both." I had to stop the word "What!" from snapping out of my mouth. Instead, I pressed my lips into a thin line and looked at her, waiting to hear the full story. When she finished, all I could think about was the fact that they went from $23,000 in car debt to $47,000 with seemingly no regard for their debt-free goals. If that wasn't enough, they used the profits from their house sale for the down payments. All that money . . . gone.

Gracefully, I did my best to tell them exactly what they needed to hear without being cruel or unprofessional. (It was tough. Their actions were a huge mistake.) I needed them to understand how much they'd set themselves back and how detrimental this type of behavior would be for their future plan. They could kiss paying off their debt in two years goodbye!

After I felt like I said what I needed to, I told them I hoped they understood why I was so hard on them, and that it wasn't out of a lack of care or sympathy. I needed them to commit! I needed them to believe in the power their commitment to the plan would have.

They both nodded slowly with downcast eyes. Then, the wife looked up and said into the camera, "I have one more question." My smile came back, and I asked, "Okay, what is it?

"Well, we have $4,000 in a sock drawer. Can we use it to buy a boat? We found a great deal!" I seriously thought it might be a prank at this point and looked around the room. Unfortunately, she was serious. Obviously, I told her there was no way that was a good idea. She nodded, and they hung up. Ouch.

The next session wasn't any better. I was a little more prepared this time, but I still heard things I didn't want to hear. They were not sticking to the budget or hitting their payoff goals. Absolutely nothing was sticking, despite the fact they walked through the Awareness and Knowledge Levels. This is why the Commitment Level is so essential to the process. It was clear that Alexis and Cody were ready to rationalize and give into more debt if it was convenient and seemed necessary.

Finally, I was fed up and said, "Do you know what I think you're going to do? You're not going to do anything I suggest. In a year or so, you're going to buy a house that's too big with a thirty-year mortgage, you're going to drop the budget, and you'll have dug yourself deeper in debt. In five years, you'll call me again to clean it up. The husband nodded, "Sounds about right." My eyes widened. I knew that was my last coaching session with them.

Cody and Alexis genuinely wanted things to change. Everyone does! They wrote out all their goals and dreamed about their future. They got out the notebook, pen, and calculator and totaled everything up. Like everyone else, they didn't want to continue living with the stress of an overdrawn bank account or multiple late fees. No one wants to be reminded daily they have no retirement savings. No one wants the shame of fore-closure or repossession. However, no one wants to make a sacrifice either. No one wants to change their lifestyle, really.

Do you see the dilemma? You're in a standoff. At this point, you have all the knowledge and you've made all the small pivots you're comfortable with. You're eating out less, you've cut expensive memberships, and maybe you've even committed (unlike Cody and Alexis) to following your budget 100 percent. But now it's time to have the courage to go big or go home. If not, there may not be a home to go back to if you don't commit to the big sacrifices that need to happen right now.

THE COURAGE TO COMMIT

Though I am sympathetic to how you were fooled into making your money mistakes whether by poor education, learned behaviors, or trauma, you can't afford to feel sorry for yourself anymore. It's time to change. Motivational speaker Adrian Rainey says,

> Committed people make a decision to be mentally tough and do the work. They have a clear picture of what they want and why they want it, but they are open to how they get it. Instead of limiting themselves to the past or being slow to adjust their approach, they learn, change, and dig deep to achieve the results they want. Committed people do whatever it takes.[2]

Isn't that true? Whatever it takes. You need to dig deep and consider the work you're really willing to put in. Is it more hours at work and fewer hours at home with the family? Is it canceling your annual vacations? Is it selling the dream house or muscle car? Is it taking your child out of private school? These are big asks, but they all can be done. It's all up to you now. No one can make this decision for you. You have got to be brave! After you make the courageous decision to cut up the credit cards or reduce your lifestyle spending, that courage turns to confidence in yourself. You'll know you can make the hard choices and stay steadfast even in financial turmoil. With this confidence, you'll gain lots of momentum. You'll challenge yourself to pay off more debt, handle more obstacles, and get through the Pyramid even faster.

My single-mom client Kathy had two teenage kids and a big financial mess. She told me she was so tired of living paycheck to paycheck and so stressed many nights she couldn't sleep. Most people get out of debt in one of three ways: (1) They cut lifestyle expenses to almost nothing, (2) they sell their assets, and/or (3) they work extra jobs. Well, Kathy had nothing to sell and her budget was already bare bones. Working another job was the only way we could boost her income and start tackling the debt that kept her up at night. Like most people, Kathy was resistant at first. However, seeing her budget laid out for the first time made her realize she had no other choice.

It took her long hours of hard work, determination, and commitment. Was it worth it? She'd tell you it was. She paid off $100,000 of debt in twenty-eight months and got her fully funded emergency fund shortly thereafter. Remember, this was all on her own! Her gains didn't stop at the emergency fund, she kept working through the Pyramid and kept her second job long enough to put a down payment on a *brand new* house.

I'll never forget meeting with her after she reached this huge milestone. She said, "I can finally quit my second job and get my weekends back! I will miss my co-workers because they were fun to be around, but I'm excited to be with my kids more and engage in my hobbies again—all in a brand new house." She paused and said, "I cannot even begin to share how much peace has been brought into my life by working with you." This is what accountability and commitment looks like.

Despite the difficulties, despite what you'll miss out on, and despite the shame of past mistakes, commitment is worth it. Remember what you dreamed about when you set goals at the start of your journey? Now is the time to commit! Now is the time to let go! Now is the time to embrace a new way of thinking, no matter how scary, no matter how unattainable it may appear. Freedom is just around the corner!

Chapter 10 Takeaways

- **Hardships are coming no matter how solid the strategy is.** Plan for the challenges that come with the Commitment Level, and you'll be equipped to tackle your hurdles.

- **Commitment is your fork-in-the-road moment.** Choose freedom over captivity. Choose joy over sorrow. Choose peace over stress. Choose victory over regret.

- **Commitment is one of the hardest things to achieve.** In order to fully commit, you have to let go of the fear of failure, the pain of an earlier experience, or something you really love.

- **Go for the big win.** Don't let false comforts keep you from financial freedom. If you're committed, you'll do whatever it takes to get there.

- **Acknowledge your financial past and start again with a clean slate and spirit of courage.** Blaming others for your current money troubles won't help you. Commitment to change will.

LEVEL FOUR

Momentum

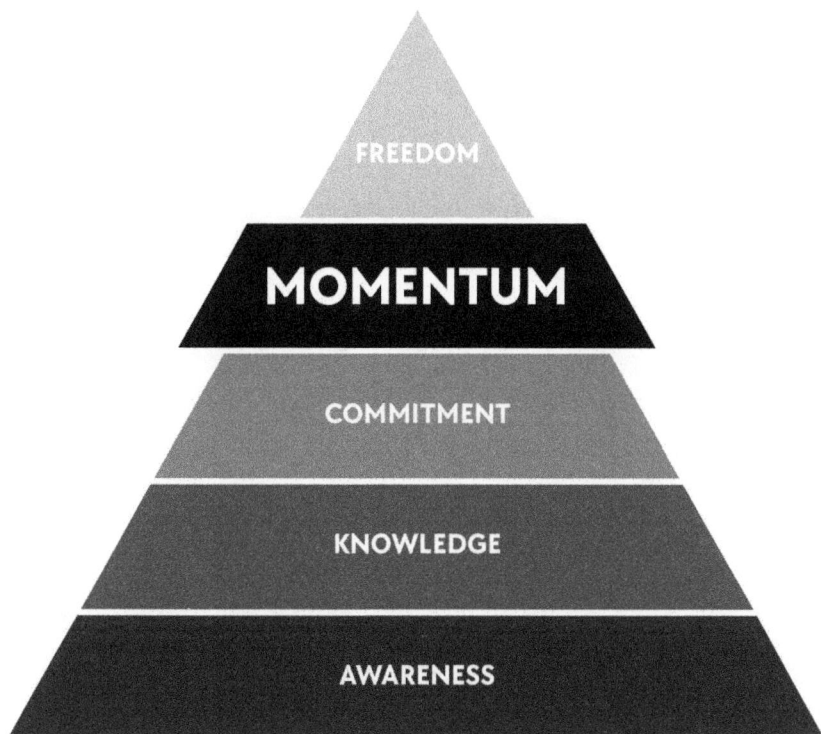

FREEDOM

MOMENTUM

COMMITMENT

KNOWLEDGE

AWARENESS

CHAPTER 11

Overcome the Four Thieves of Momentum

Keep moving ahead because action creates momentum, which in turn creates unanticipated opportunities.

—*Nick Vujicic,*
Life Without Limits

REACHING THE MOMENTUM LEVEL is an exciting time. You're hitting significant goals you've set like saving up your emergency fund, paying off a few debts, increasing your income, and maybe finally getting the IRS off your back. Whatever it is, you're full of fire and drive to go forward. However, when you first commit to your financial plan, things may be both tough and slow. You'll probably fail at following your budget a few times and second-guess some of your big sacrifices, but what you learned in the previous chapters will help you persevere and get through the hard times. When you're on Levels One, Two, and Three, you're in the mud, and you're fighting every step of the way. You can't see the finish line but can only conceptualize that it's there.

But when you hit Level Four, Momentum, things finally get easier for you and the Financial Freedom Pyramid's summit comes into view.

Seeing that summit, your heart will start pounding a little faster and new energy will jolt through your body. Clients tell me all the time how they run for those goals once they actually get them in sight. If you were climbing a mountain and could finally see the peak, even if your legs were sore and you were considering turning back, you never would if you saw how close you were to that beautiful view . . . and that's what your end goal is, right? Beautiful!

My clients start out stressed and struggling and tempted to give up. Tempted to back out on their commitment and return to those comfortable bad habits and live in their familiar prison. But when they stick with it and use my strategies to go all in, they get that first meaningful, motivating victory to charge them forward. For some, it's getting that $1,000 emergency fund saved up fast. For others, it's paying off their kid's musical instruments. Honestly, for some it's just going one week without an overdraft notice. Whatever it is, their small win pushes them forward and shows them they actually can do this. Seriously, I think many of my clients are convinced they'll fail until they reach this point. But with their first win, they truly believe in themselves and the system they're committed to. That first win leads to bigger wins like paying off the car until they reach the final level on the Pyramid.

But I'd be lying to you if I told you that Level Four was without any threats. You need to be aware of the Four Thieves of Momentum. These thieves slow your progress and, in some cases, cause you to restart the Cycle of Regret. They sneak in and prevent you from moving forward and believing in yourself, turning your hope again into a vain wish. As these thieves break into your financial plan, you can fend them off smartly with the help of your accountability partner and your newly learned financial principles. Be aware of these thieves that S.L.O.W. you down and threaten your path to freedom:

Situational Principles
Life Circumstances
Out of Gas
Weak Results

SITUATIONAL PRINCIPLES

We spent the Knowledge Level of the Pyramid breaking down the essential principles you need to be successful with this plan. These included the seven proven biblical principles of finance and the first three Baby Steps. If you keep these principles close to you, you'll know what to do when faced with a financial challenge. Not sticking close to these principles, however, will send you right back into the Cycle of Regret.

Too often I see clients with "situational principles," which means they stick to the values and systems when they're convenient and easy ... but they make exceptions in certain circumstances. For instance, I worked with a couple who had done incredible work on Levels One through Three of the Pyramid. In fact, they were flying through the Momentum Level as well. After trying multiple times to get their finances in order, they'd found this program and an accountability partner (me) to help them stick to it. They'd paid off $85,000 of their $100,000 debt and were so close to the Freedom Level they could almost touch it. They had completed Baby Step 1, were at the end of Baby Step 2, and as they got nearer to closing that gap, I eagerly awaited that big victory session where we could celebrate such a massive debt payoff and catapult into Baby Step 3.

However, the joyful session never came. In one of our final meetings, when they were 85 percent complete with their debt-free journey, they told me they'd financed two fairly new cars. They decided, despite the principles we'd established and agreed upon, that debt on reliable transportation was okay. They said they *needed* safe transportation for their situation and were tricked into thinking a newer car would somehow be cheaper in the long run.[1] Because of this "need," and because they worked hard, they decided they deserved a vehicle spending spree. Their choice to finance these newer cars was devastating to the couple's goals. It plunged them back into significant debt and for no good reason other than, "I want it now, so I'll rationalize it."

My wife and I almost did something similar. We desperately wanted a larger, nicer house. However, right when we were finally ready to purchase a newer one, housing prices shot up and priced us out of the market.

Instead of taking that as our sign that it wasn't our time to buy a house, for some reason (note the sarcasm here), we requested the mortgage lender run the numbers with a twenty-year mortgage. We saw that adjusted payment and, oh, was it tempting. We could make that payment. And since it was a twenty-year mortgage and not a thirty-year mortgage, we still thought we were doing better than most people and were only making a *tiny* compromise. Notice the rationalization here? It was only five years different from the fifteen-year mortgage. No big deal, right? Yet, after making that small compromise, we made the decision to get pre-approved for a thirty-year loan, which then led us to look at homes in a higher price range. Yeah, we were about to have a ton of debt and a one-way ticket back into the Cycle of Regret.

Look how far that tiny compromise took us. We were like the frog in the proverbial pot of water. If you put a frog into boiling hot water, it will quickly jump out. However, when you put a frog into a pot full of room temperature water and slowly turn up the heat, you will have frog legs later that night. The frog won't even know it's being cooked alive. That's what happens when you have situational principles. Each small step in the other direction eventually adds up, and the next thing you know, you're drowning in debt again.

Fortunately, we had good accountability partners and gave ourselves some time to think before we made such a stupid decision. We thought back to all the pain we'd gone through because of our past financial mistakes and agreed we'd never go back there. At that moment while contemplating that twenty-year mortgage, we were really tempted to compromise our principles based on wanting the bigger and better house right now, but the parts of life where principles really matter are in the tough decisions. I'm so glad we didn't fall into that trap and set ourselves behind in our goals by buying a larger home we couldn't afford. Instead, we decided to remodel our current home using cash (so no added guilt of new debt) and now live contented in our updated home.

LIFE CIRCUMSTANCES

Another thief of momentum is tough life circumstances. A single-mom client named Brynn had just arrived at the Momentum Level. She was seeing progress, and it was helping her gain tons of traction every week that launched her closer and closer to her goals. However, Brynn, the sole money-maker in her house, had unexpected surgery that took her out of work for a few months. This meant she'd be low on funds and unable to do her side gigs. Plus, her health was still uncertain after surgery, so she had no idea how long she'd be out of work.

My recommendation was she pause the plan. Yes, you can do that! You can pause the plan as long as pausing doesn't mean you go back into debt or stop budgeting. Pausing the plan means you go back to paying the minimum on your debt payments and pour everything you can into savings, or, in Brynn's case, use everything you've got to stay afloat and out of debt while recovering from surgery. Brynn was very discouraged, feeling like she'd never get out of debt and terrified the situation would set her back. I loved that she was aware of the cost of "waiting," but there are times in life when your dream financial future isn't the top priority. Brynn needed to focus on her health and her family. And because of the hard work she'd already done, the recovery wasn't as stressful as it could have been. She had a few debts out of the way and that starter emergency fund was there to support her.

I worked with another couple who took in their three nephews when their mother suddenly became unfit to care for them. They'd just started meeting with me and had a good plan in place, but now they had not one kid, but four. The kids came with nothing and the couple wasn't certain if the boys would be with them for a few weeks or forever (turned out to be forever), so they had a lot of immediate needs. As they got everything sorted out and found resources, they paused the plan, buckled down on budgeting, and pushed through the chaos. A couple months in, they were able to restart the plan and were thankful for the budgeting habits they'd started before their family doubled in size.

These circumstances are hard for someone who has already committed to their financial goals because now something is actually preventing them from moving forward like they want to. It's like they're shackled. When they're finally let loose, time has passed and their goal is further away. This can be so demoralizing it stops them from moving forward at all. Don't let this happen! A quick pause doesn't undo all your progress, it only delays it for a minute. It's like when you warm up food in the microwave but then get side-tracked. Once you come back, the food is still there and perfectly good, you've just got to zap it one more time. You still have all the opportunity in front of you, you simply need a little fire. The best way to start that fire is to restart the plan and hit your next new checkpoint.

Knowing when it's time to take a break will involve discernment. I also recommend meeting with your accountability partner to discuss whether it's truly a pause-worthy problem. Things like job loss, death, pregnancy, and illness are all big ones that can definitely warrant entering "survival mode." However, there might be other big-for-you problems I haven't listed here. When something comes up, look for wisdom, be practical, and stick to your principles no matter what.

OUT OF GAS

For some people, momentum continues to build as they're knocking down debts and building up their savings. For others, the momentum slows as they encounter some of their bigger debts. They go from paying debts of a few thousand dollars each, to trying to pay off their five- or six-figure student loan bill, and get discouraged and completely run out of gas. When this happens, people want to give up. They accept what they've accomplished up to that point as all they'll be able to muster and decide that this big debt is going to stick around like a feral cat they once fed—except it's not cute anymore. It's annoying now. But either way, it's here to stay.

You might call this situation "burnout," where you work hard but don't think you're making progress—and I totally get this mentality. With burnout, you feel like you can't go on. However, most people aren't burned-out, but fatigued. What you're really experiencing is fatigue from working hard *while* you're making progress. You're just tired and you need something to refuel your gas tank. To power through the rest of the Momentum Level, here are some refueling ideas:

- **Reward** yourself for smaller checkpoints, like getting yourself a DQ Blizzard for every $2,000 you pay off. (Most expensive Blizzard ever, right?)
- **Recalibrate** your budget and goals to see if faster debt payoff is possible.
- **Revisit** your why and remind yourself how close you are to your goals.
- **Reevaluate** your situation with your accountability partner and look for advice and encouragement.
- **Reunite** with others on the same journey to bond over the hardship and move forward in comradery.
- **Reset** new realistic short-term goals that you can hit fast.
- **Restore** your hope for success by talking with people who have completed the Pyramid.
- **Review** how far you've come instead of how far you have to go.

Let's stay with this last one for a minute: Review how far you've come instead of how far you have to go. It can be easy at this stage to get filled with guilt and shame over the financial mistakes that put you in this predicament. Once you learn about the principles of personal finance and how long it might take you to reach financial freedom, it's normal to mourn what you've lost. Even when you're making progress, it's easy to focus on what you're *not* doing and what you *haven't* done. Dan Sullivan has a whole book on this called *The Gap and the Gain*,[2] which focuses on the psychological factors that prevent us from getting to our ideal life.

If you only visualize the distance between the starting point and the finish line, you'll get discouraged. However, when you flip the script and focus, not on the distance between where you are now and your final goal, but on the distance between where you were and what you've accomplished so far, you'll see significant gain. I'll give you a real-world example. When my clients get their emergency fund saved up and start paying off extra debt, they feel energized and motivated to race for their goals. But, more often than not, they get hit with an unexpected expense like a car repair or a medical bill. When this happens, they have to use their emergency fund and can't put extra toward debt, and for many, this is deflating. All they see is what they "lost," but I see what they gained! Each time a client tells me of their unexpected expense and looks defeated, I ask them, "So . . . if this hit you a year or two ago, what would you have done to handle it?" My clients always say, "Oh, man. I don't even want to think about what I would've done." Then they list off credit cards, personal loans, or other forms of debt.

Recently, I was working with a couple who had a decent income, but like the average American household, had enough debt to fill a pro-football stadium. However, no situation is beyond fixing, so we made a plan and the couple was incredibly motivated to tackle their debt in the time frame I laid out. They'd get through the Pyramid in just a couple of years and were so excited to "get their life back." Well, the first three months didn't go as planned—at all! The first month, they had two expensive appliances go out. No more dishwasher or washing machine. Not only did they have to make a budget for replacements, but they had to hand wash dishes and drive to a laundromat every few days while they saved up. I bet swiping that credit card was really tempting after they lugged home sopping wet laundry because they didn't bring enough quarters to finish drying the last load. I get that this is a first-world problem, but what a nightmare.

The next month, they had over $1,000 in car repairs. These weren't as a result of negligence either. Everything seemed to fall apart at once, and even after suggesting they get multiple quotes, the estimate was still a grand. Unfortunately, their hard season didn't end there. A routine trip to the dentist revealed their daughter needed braces. Honestly, when I heard this, I thought they'd want to give up. They'd been hit by almost every thief of momentum before they really got started. We figured out how to cover every expense, but things were tight, extra hours at work were long, and the starter emergency fund was drained.

During one session I asked them, "How are you guys doing? You haven't been able to pay off any debt in the first ninety days." The husband cheerfully responded, "We're doing great! Yes, we're bummed that we haven't paid off any debt, but the fact that we've been able to use cash for these expenses without incurring any more debt is incredible! Had all of this happened months earlier, we would've been sunk." And they were absolutely right. Wow! My clients were reminding *me* of the gap versus gain principle.

Don't forget how far you've come. Be sure to measure your progress in every way. Document what you've done and have an accountability partner that will always celebrate those wins with you and remind you of your accomplishments. Don't think about the gap, think about the gain. Focus on the successes, not the failures of the past. This is a game-changing way of thinking and will help you with all your goals. (I highly recommend you read Dan Sullivan's book.)

Measuring how far you've come will give you fuel to continue on. It will give you hope to stick it out. Finding other people with stories like yours will inspire you to believe reaching your goals is possible. After meeting with thousands of clients, I can tell you, in many areas of your life, this is absolutely possible.

WEAK RESULTS

Depending on your situation, results can feel minimal, and that could stall your motivation in the same way running out of gas stalls your vehicle's momentum. If you're only contributing $200–$300 toward debt every month, yet you have $100,000 of debt that needs cleaning up, your contributions can feel like using a Dixie cup of water to put out a forest fire.

Years ago I met with a couple who had six figures of consumer debt, and they hired me to help them formulate a plan to get out of it. They had nothing to sell and had cut back on all the expenses they could. The only other option available to pay off this debt quickly was working side hustles.

It is a given that most people would prefer not to work a second job, and this couple was no exception. When I brought up a second job as a potential option, the couple was aghast that I would even suggest it. They went on to tell me how important family time is with their children for the few short years they have them at home. I explained that I understood the importance of family time. As a parent of five children myself, I understand how precious those years are, and the sacrifice I was asking them to consider. However, I also understood that being deep in debt would make it harder to provide for their children, especially when they got started as adults.

With the side-hustle option being a non-negotiable, I explained that if they lived on the budget and used the debt snowball method, they could still pay off this mountain of debt in five years. Granted they could have paid it off in half the time with the side hustles, but that was not an option they were willing to employ. And shortly thereafter, the coaching program they were enrolled in had come to an end.

Interestingly enough, they called me five years later to see what I could do to help, as they were still six figures in debt. To be fair, they did reduce their debt some, but not a lot. As I reviewed their budget and potential options for getting rid of their debt, the option of getting a side hustle was still the prescription. And, five years later, they still used family time as the reason why they wouldn't budge on getting an extra job.

I explained to them directly, without being mean, that there was a plan in place to pay off the debt five years ago that they didn't follow through with. It wasn't to shame them, but to let them know their way of doing things was not getting the results they wanted. Then I said, "If you don't treat getting out of debt with urgency and intensity, in five years you're going to reject working an extra job because of family time again, except this time you will have teenagers wanting cars and going to prom.

"Five years from then" I continued, "you will want to help pay their college expenses and five years later, you'll want to help with their wedding expenses. And five years after that, there will be grandchildren you'll want to spoil. Eventually, you'll end up at retirement, still in debt with no peace, all because of family time that could have been sacrificed for only two and half years max."

As your financial coach, I can't stress this enough: if you want to reach your goal of financial freedom, nothing should be off the table, and if there is something you can't or won't budge on, you need to find something comparable to take its place. Otherwise, you're still going to struggle because of your small contributions and momentum will drop. To make your contributions bigger, get another job, sell stuff, rent out a room, donate plasma, start charging your kids for hugs. (Okay, that one won't work). But the point is do whatever it takes to give yourself enough fuel to reach the end. And with higher contributions to your goals, more momentum will come.

Mary, a single mom I worked with, wanted two things: (1) to get out of debt in two years and (2) to stop working her second job as soon as possible. When I met her, she looked completely frazzled and overwhelmed. She'd been trying to work towards debt freedom for a while, but had completely run out of gas. Together we worked on the budget, and I made a plan for her that would allow her to get out of debt in two years *if* she kept her second job.

This was not what she wanted to hear, and her eyes welled with tears. She said, "Justin, I can't. I don't have it in me anymore. I want to spend more time with my daughter." My heart ached for her. It really did. I remembered missing a lot of my kids' activities and events when we were getting out of debt. I knew exactly how she felt, and I told her that. However, I also knew if she settled for less than going all the way with the plan, she'd get comfortable with her partial success, and eventually she'd be back with me in tears deep in the Cycle of Regret. If she stuck it out, Mary would not only find the peace and joy of her realized dreams, but of her daughter's too. She'd be able to buy the two-story playhouse, go for a spontaneous McDonald's lunch date, and book that trip to her favorite theme park with all the princess extras. Being able to say yes so much more in the future meant, for now, Mary had to say no. She had to say no to quitting her job and spending more time at home ... for a little while.

I gave her my pep talk, and then said, "Mary, with the new budget that entire paycheck from the second job is going to debt. So ..."

"So, you're saying I can quit my job in two years, because I'll be debt-free?" A glimmer of hope shone in her tearful eyes.

"Bingo!" I said. "You've been working that second job with no end in sight. That sounds hopeless to me too. But now we've a set date when you can quit."

I asked her if she could commit to her budget and her second job for ninety days. She agreed, and each month, she was more energized and less burdened by her situation. Her debt was melting away and she got a taste of freedom from those big results, giving her confidence and hope, which also influenced other areas of life like her decision to quit smoking. The results of her commitment made all the difference to refill her tank and fuel her towards her goals.

Throughout Chapter 7 there were multiple success stories of how my clients got out of debt to obtain financial freedom. To summarize, they increased income through extra jobs or overtime, cut expenses down to the bone, sold everything in sight, or did a combination of these options. If you want to gain momentum like those clients did, you'll need to come to terms with what it will take to reach your financial goals. If you're still struggling with this, feel free to be creative. Make a game out of it. The goal is to create action that leads to momentum.

I sometimes create what I call stretch goals with my clients to push them one step further that they think they can go. For example, a client might have $900 to put towards their smallest debt, but they need $1,000 to pay it off. I'll ask them to go back to their budget and see where they can find an extra $100 to pay off the debt one month ahead of schedule. Often, because the smaller goal (or checkpoint) is within reach, they're willing to sacrifice a little bit more to achieve faster results.

KEEP FORWARD MOMENTUM

To combat the Four Thieves, you need to have a plan to overcome them. Commit 100 percent to your principles. Decide how you'll refuel when life happens and you run out of gas. Adopt a "gain versus gap" mindset, and make sure you supercharge your efforts to maximize your results. As you go through the Momentum level, you may encounter setbacks, temptations, and other hard stuff. Be prepared for it and make sure your accountability partner or coach is prepared too. They'll be one of the key components that get you out of your rut and set you on the path toward freedom again.

A sound financial plan with accountability will change your perspective and help you stay focused on the Pyramid. We can't return to the Cycle of Regret now! The finish line is in sight. Keep your eyes on that end goal and don't let any thief steal your chance of receiving the financial freedom that awaits you ahead.

Chapter 11 Takeaways

- **Avoid situational principles.** Commit 100 percent to the financial principles you learned from the Knowledge Level. This will help you know what to do when faced with a financial challenge and avoid the Cycle of Regret.

- **Overcome life circumstances.** A pause to your financial plan doesn't undo all your progress. We all have situations that interrupt progress. Relax, restart the plan, and hit your next new checkpoint.

- **Refuel your emotional and mental gas tank.** Power through the rest of the Momentum Level using these refueling ideas: reward yourself, recalibrate your budget, revise your why, reevaluate your situation, reunite with others, reset your goals, restore your hope, and review how far you've come.

- **Eliminate weak results.** If you feel you're losing momentum because of small contributions to your goals, make the contributions bigger. Consider every possibility and do whatever it will take to keep the momentum going.

- **Practice a "gain" mindset.** Document everything you've done, and your accountability partner will celebrate those wins with you and remind you of your accomplishments. Don't think about the gap, think about the gain. Measuring how far you've come will give you fuel to continue on and hope to stick it out.

LEVEL FIVE

Freedom

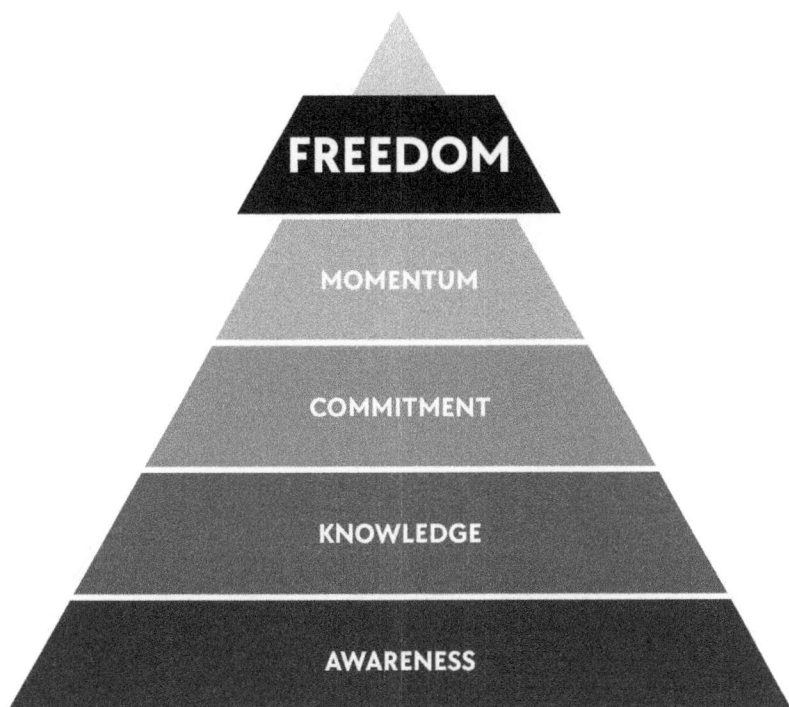

CHAPTER 12

Finding Hope on Every Level

What you get by achieving your goals is not as important as what you become by achieving your goals.

—Zig Ziglar,
See You At the Top

FREEDOM IS HERE! It's time to let go of the balloons, launch the confetti, play the music, and celebrate. What you've done so far calls for cheering, dancing, and screaming "I'm free!" You might even get a few noise complaints from the neighbors (just kidding). Seriously, all your friends should know what you've done and the relief and joy on your face should be clear to everyone. You've done what you once thought impossible. Because of your commitment to the plan, you are now reaping the rewards of your improved money habits.

You may laugh a little while reading that because you're probably still on the early levels of the Pyramid. You're still in the thick of it! You look around and don't see a lot worth celebrating, especially if you've sold most of the things in your house and had to budget-cut a favorite weekend activity.

Right now, instead of seeing success, you only see sacrifice. Earlier, I told you financial freedom is not a one-size-fits-all destination. But the big climactic close, where you hit all the goals you set in the beginning and live on a comfortable retirement in the end, isn't the only time you'll feel hope and relief. You taste freedom all throughout the process, which motivates you toward the finish line.

This is so important for you to understand. I don't want you to think this entire process is no fun and no frills. As you go through each level of the Pyramid, you'll taste so much joy and hope as you get closer to the top, that even while things are tough, you'll know exactly why you keep going. When you feel that hope for the future and the joy of breaking free from one habit, one debt, or one negative thought, you've won. Chase the taste of that freedom all the way to the big feast of freedom at the end and remember that at the beginning of every success is sacrifice.

THE PYRAMID GIVES HOPE

In the last chapter we talked about the gap and the gain. If you're having a hard time refueling on the Momentum Level and the lack of drive is threatening to end your journey, look back and see how far you've come. Looking back on your progress can be extremely motivating, even if the finish line is still far away. Think about this: The gap and the gain implies that there *are* gains. There are wins that show up throughout the process and these provide hope, ensuring you never return to the Cycle of Regret. Hope is powerful, and with every step of this process, you'll find it. But without a plan, there is no hope. Proverbs 29:18 says where there is no vision, the people perish, and that's absolutely true. With a plan, with a vision, there is hope. It's that simple.

So, even if you've just started this process, there's already a taste of freedom, already hope. Your future goals and dreams are secured. Because of hope, they're locked in and ready for you to arrive at them. Of course, not everything will come at once and some dreams are tougher to reach than others, but the point is as long as you stay on the plan, even when you're moving slowly and experiencing setbacks, total financial freedom isn't a wish on a star. It's a certain future. You've made it a reality simply by taking the first step forward.

EMOTION SCALE

1	2	3	4	5	6	7	8	9	10
Hopeless	-	Overwhelmed	-	Stressed	-	Hopeful	-	Confident	-	Peaceful

Back in Chapter 1, I introduced you to a scale I use with my clients to measure their emotions attached to their current financial situation. On average, when my clients begin working with me, they rate themselves somewhere between a two and a four. Over the next six months, I guide my clients through the Pyramid and those same clients, on average, rate themselves between a seven and a nine. This can be you if you stay committed to this process. Let this give you hope as you progress through your journey to financial freedom.

We laugh about it now, but one of the hardest parts of my debt-free journey, where I almost lost sight of the finish line, happened over a decade ago on my daughter, Julia's, birthday. We were in the thick of our journey, and we almost never went out to eat. However, to celebrate the occasion, we gave our daughter the option of getting a gift or going out to dinner, and she eagerly chose to eat out. So, with a fifty-dollar budget, we packed up all five kids and headed to a restaurant called Hickory Park. Julia really wanted to go there because she'd get free ice cream and "Happy Birthday" sung to her. She'd get the most bang for her birthday buck.

As we sat down to order, I quickly scanned the menu to determine how we were all going to eat within budget. With some quick mental math, I figured it all out. Jessica and I would each get a basic entrée and water, and each kid would get a kid's meal and water—except the birthday girl. She could have her favorite soft drink. After tax and tip, we'd still be under budget.

But Julia was running her finger over the appetizer section, exploring the options and my shoulders tightened up a bit. Sure enough, she looked up at me with her big brown eyes and asked, "Dad, can we get cheese balls?" She was sweet and polite. There was no attitude or threatening tween glares you might expect from a nine-year-old. Of course, this made it harder. There was literally no extra money anywhere, and though I loved Julia very much, I would not swipe our debit card for something outside of the budget. Though she couldn't understand it, compromising the budget would mean compromising the vision we had for our family's future. It would mean stepping off the plan and turning financial freedom from a certainty to a fantasy. It sounds silly—it was only cheese balls! But at that moment, I kept my mind focused on the family vacations, her first car, and the buckets of cheese balls I'd be able to provide for her in the future if we stuck to it, and regretfully said, "Sorry, sweetheart, no cheese balls."

"But Dad?" She batted her eyelashes and gave a pleading smile.

"No, we can't get cheese balls, but remember, you're getting ice cream and a birthday song." I said the last part enthusiastically, hoping she'd feel like the ice cream was bigger and better than cheese balls. Her pleading smile dropped to a frown and her head hung, staring at the golden cheese balls displayed on the menu.

I felt horrible. What dad wouldn't let their daughter have cheese balls on her birthday? Especially Hickory Park's locally famous, delicious fried balls of cheese. The night went on, everyone happily ate, and Julia got her ice cream. But from then on, I never forgot I denied my daughter cheese balls. However, I continued to gain hope through the Pyramid. I could count dozens of wins and still make out our promising future. As long as I stayed on the plan, someday I wouldn't have to think about having margin in the budget for cheese balls. This gave me so much hope in that tough season.

I share this story because I feel like this is where a lot of you are right now. Of course, you'd *love* to go on a big vacation, remodel your whole house, and give like crazy, but these things don't keep you up at night. What does keep you up at night is saying no to the pricey event your friends invited you to, living with your broken dishwasher instead of fixing it, or not getting your kid cheese balls on their special day. I see your daily struggle, but know this: Hope climbs with each level of the Pyramid.

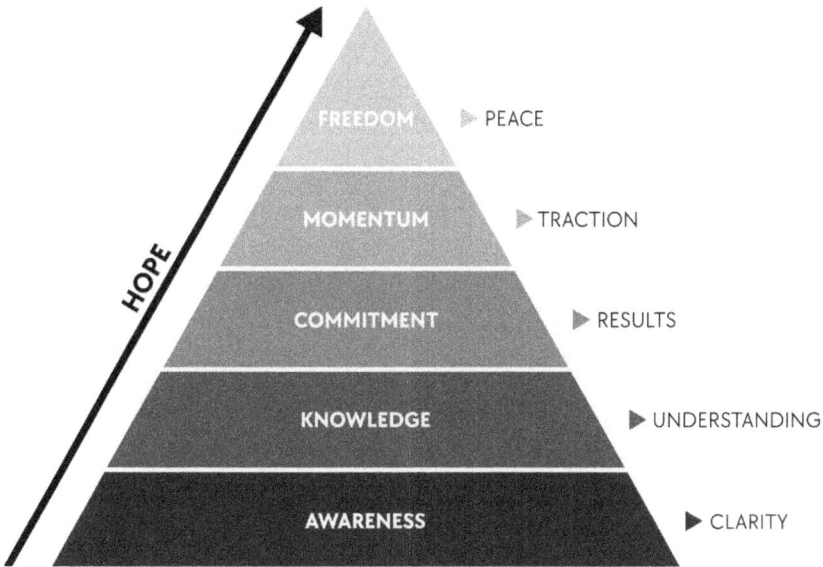

HOPE IN AWARENESS

I'm going to be honest, finding hope on this first level is hard! You're as early as you can be in your journey, farthest away from the finish line than on any other level. You now know the full extent of your financial mess and you have become intimately aware of all your past mistakes. All your bad habits have become clearly defined and you know the road ahead will be tough. So, where's the hope?

Hope at the Awareness Level is more tangible than you think. There's such a feeling of triumph when you finally do what you've been scared to do all those years. When you finally open all those accounts, total those debts, and get a sense of your monthly deficit, you do something powerful. You triumph over fear because you now have faith in the future. Anxiety about your financial mess lingers and eats at you for as long as you allow your mess to stay hidden in the dark. When you finally bring it to light, you'll find relief—even if the reality is worse than you thought—because now you know where you're at financially.

Once you know the truth, there are no more secrets or skeletons in the closet, so you can move forward. You've broken free from your first chain. And if you could break this chain, don't you think you can do more? There's so much hope here! Second Timothy 1:7 says, "For God gave us a spirit not of fear, but of power and love and self-control." Isn't that what we're talking about here? This is how you climb the Pyramid—with this God-given power, love, and self-control.

HOPE IN KNOWLEDGE

As someone who likes numbers, I like clear answers. I like one way to solve a problem. However, with financial issues, it doesn't feel like there is one answer. It feels like there are dozens of options out there and none of them say the same thing. The Knowledge Level can be paralyzing and send you early into that Cycle of Regret if you don't know what to do once you realize you have a problem.

However, when you use this proven, research-backed plan supported by thousands of testimonies, you'll have confidence you're on the right track. There's hope when you *know* a plan works. Then, it's only a matter of following it. With clear instructions, you don't doubt you can assemble that new bookcase or your kid's bike. However, without a manual, you'll be constantly anxious and feeling hopeless throughout the process because you don't have proof that what you're doing will result in the finished product.

On the Knowledge Level, you have hope because you have proof of the finished product. With every financial move you make, the Baby Steps have clear, verified answers. There's no fear that your decisions will continue to set you back, to perpetuate your paycheck to paycheck prison, and to leave you stressed and overwhelmed. You are free from that on the

Knowledge Level because you know where you're going, and this how-to map will get you there.

HOPE IN COMMITMENT

Here's where the real hope comes in. A lot of the hope we've talked about in the last two sections is all about feelings, which is good. Your financial mess has your mind in a grip of constant stress, so the relief and hope you feel at the Awareness and Knowledge Levels are essential. But now? Now you get to see the real fruit of your actions. On the Commitment Level, you buckle down and do what needs to be done to get through the Pyramid fast.

This is where a lot of people hire a financial coach or get an accountability partner, because someone to push you forward on your goal of commitment makes your efforts even more fruitful. An accountability partner is like having a new superpower of hope and energy for reaching your goals. According to a study by the Association of Talent Development,[1] you'll be 95 percent more likely to succeed if you are accountable to a third party.

I coached a couple with three kids who were at the end of their rope. The wife, Rachel, had her salary significantly reduced and her husband, John, worked as a real estate agent with extremely variable income. They had $57,000 in debt that included car loans, credit cards, student loans, and a home equity line of credit (HELOC). They felt like they had no way to tackle this debt.

Not only did they want help with paying off the debt, but they also wanted a better process of managing their money and a third party to hold them accountable to reach their goals. That's where I came in. As we started working together, they overcame their behavioral and emotional struggles and, as their hope grew, got a taste of freedom on those first couple levels. They committed to me as their accountability partner and paid off their debt in one year. From that commitment, they were able to use all the extra money they had to fully fund their emergency fund (Baby Step 3) and pay *in cash* for a family cruise.

A single-mom client with three kids I worked with was in the thick of her divorce and had $22,000 in consumer debt as well as a house she could no longer afford on her own. Talk about being stressed! After meeting with me, we decided selling the house was her best option, and because she was committed to the process, she went for it. She found another house with a fifteen-year fixed-rate mortgage and got to work. She got a second part-time job (that she actually ended up loving) and paid off all of her debt in six months. Truly, getting debt-free gave her a fresh start and a ton of confidence coming out of her painful divorce.

The Dawson's are another couple that recently paid off all their debt, so now all of their extra money is going to a down payment for a house. When they came to me, they had $31,000 in debt and paid it all off in ten months. Now that's commitment! The fire in their bellies and the urgency to become debt-free motivated the husband to look into other jobs. He found a better paying job, much more fulfilling than his old one, and it allowed them to pay off their debt extremely fast. After that, they didn't stop. They got their three to six month living-expenses fund saved in the bank in ninety days. The hope they felt all the way through each level drove them miles from the Cycle of Regret and launched them full speed to true freedom.

Here's one more story to get you hyped. I need you to know how possible financial freedom is. Twenty-one-year-old Logan had $50,000 in debt. Once we walked through the Awareness and Knowledge Levels, Logan said, "I thought I knew everything about personal finance and then I took the pill—like the one in the Matrix. My mind was opened to everything I was doing wrong. It seriously looked like a magic spell had been broken." Suddenly, Logan looked at his whole financial picture differently, and he pushed through the Commitment Level by making a big sacrifice: He sold his dream car. He had a Tesla with a whopping $822 monthly payment, and he used all that money to pay off debt. One year later, he said to me, "I'm so glad I hired a coach and went through the program. It changed my life for the better times one hundred! Not only can I spend with more freedom and peace, but I can give too, which is so cool to me."

Do you see the hope these people felt by committing fully to the process? Once they added in accountability, they became like an unstoppable wrecking ball through their journey, hurdling at lightning speed toward all their goals.

HOPE IN MOMENTUM

As you can see, hope increases as you go through the Pyramid and so do your tastes of freedom. And what's the cure for the Cycle of Regret? What ensures that you never fall back to your old ways? What keeps you going even when things get hard? Hope! That's what makes this process so powerful, and once you step onto the Momentum Level, that hope compounds. One victory rolls right into another victory as you knock down debt. That snowball effect is real and as your goals come closer, the reality of freedom becomes clearer and clearer.

On the Momentum Level, not only do you feel relief and see the power of your commitment, but you actually start seeing the financial gain. You see those debt numbers go way down, your savings go way up, and your flexible income increase. Many of your monthly bills will be gone as well as their minimum payments, and because of that, you get to decide where your money goes. It packs a much bigger punch when piled onto one debt after another. Many of the people I listed demolished their debt in under three years. Why? Hope from the Momentum Level became so real, they just couldn't stop.

My client Vanessa didn't feel the sense of hope as strongly on the Commitment Level, but it did come at the Momentum Level. Vanessa had $24,000 of student loans. She really wanted to get them paid off, but just couldn't see how. She was still hopeless and fearful. I walked her through her options, and we discovered she could pay off all of her debt easily in two years. However, I really pushed her to commit to the plan, get a second job, and do it in one year. At first, she declined and told me she was fine with two years, but once she started rolling and experienced victory after victory, the hope and taste of freedom persuaded her to go even faster. She got a second job and paid it all off in ten months.

Once she got her fully funded emergency fund, she took her mom on a surprise two-week winter vacation to Arizona—and paid for it all in cash! This was true freedom for Vanessa, but it didn't stop there. After she got back from vacation, she quit her second job, and her current nine-to-five, moved back to her hometown, and started a job with way less stress. She is truly living out her goals. It's not a picture-perfect Maui retirement or a $200,000 sports car, but it's empowering, hopeful, and completely freeing.

HOPE IN FREEDOM

Here's the thing, true freedom does come. Once you arrive at the top of the Pyramid, you'll be debt-free with a fully funded emergency fund of three to six months of living expenses, like Vanessa. This will give you an incredible amount of satisfaction, confidence, and peace. Those big dreams and goals you set are not only possible, but something you could make happen right here, right now, on this Freedom Level. No more waiting! As long as you have it budgeted, you can go on vacations, buy the new toys, get that car, and repurchase that $500 a month luxury gym membership. (Still can't get over that one!) Doesn't that feel like freedom? Doesn't that feel like hope? Imagine how free you'd feel. You could go to your friend's destination wedding, fix that dishwasher, and get those cheese balls.

If you find this hard to believe, remember that the average person pays upwards of $1,600 in debt payments every month, not counting their mortgage. But by the time you arrive at Level Five, the Freedom Level, your debt will be gone, and you'll have gotten a raise of almost $20,000 per year, more or less. That's worth celebrating, right? That's enough money to get started on any one of your dream goals, and those small, day-to-day challenges you struggled with become an afterthought at best. The budget works and your extra money is spent on what you prioritize.

This truth became so clear to me when I was speaking a few years ago at a conference and brought up the cheese balls story. Although it was something trivial, it was genuinely one of the most eye-opening and difficult situations I'd found myself in through our journey. My daughter, Julia, happened to be in the audience that day and heard me tell the story. She'd actually forgotten about that part of her birthday dinner and was really moved by how much that moment hurt me.

She approached me after the conference with a sly smile on her face and said, "Dad, just saying . . . you *do* owe me cheese balls."

I grinned, and we got in the car and went straight to Hickory Park for some cheese balls. While on our spontaneous date, I asked her if all the times I had to say no were worth it to her in the long run. This question was important to me because everything my coaching system is based on is the idea that it *is* worth it. The freedom to go on this spontaneous date without any financial fear, stress, or doubt was worth it. I felt it, but I needed to know she felt it too.

Without hesitation, she said, "Oh, Dad, a hundred percent." She told me she could see the fruit of not only the strict budgeting, but also the long hours I spent at work, the opportunities she had to miss, the hand-me-down clothes she had to wear, and the basically empty house we lived in after everything was sold and pushed out the door. (Okay, maybe not empty, but we did sell a lot.) Though there were lots of times I felt like a crummy dad because of all that I was doing, the ability to take an unexpected trip to a restaurant for more cheese balls than we could ever eat, affirmed that the grind was worth it. Incredibly worth it, and not just for me, but for everyone in the family. Everyone sacrificed in those days, and now a few short years later, we have reached true financial freedom.

There's a lot more you can do with an additional $20,000 than order cheese balls, but you get where I'm going. The freedom you achieve here on Level Five is real, and it'll fill you with tremendous peace. No matter what you face, you'll know that you have the awareness, knowledge, commitment, and momentum to drive you to success despite the sacrifice. It's all worth it, and it's a time for celebration.

BONUS: HOPE IN ACCOUNTABILITY

Remember Greg and Lisa? They were the couple who went to Cancun on a credit card and then wished they hadn't. Greg worked with a good friend of theirs and shared with him how much accountability with a financial coach made all the difference in breaking their Cycle of Regret and staying on track. Hearing how much financial coaching was beneficial to Greg and Lisa, this friend and his wife, Caleb and Tanya, reached out to me to get that same level of accountability. (Fun fact: Both families are competitive, so it became a race to see who would become debt-free first.)

Caleb and Tanya paid off $174,000 of debt in fourteen months! They didn't just sacrifice in one area. They sacrificed in all areas. They had two auto loans totaling $57,000 at $1,200 per month. They sold both vehicles (including the husband's dream truck) and got more affordable, but still reliable, transportation. The husband worked overtime . . . a lot of overtime. And, lastly, they sold their house. Caleb and Tanya had enough equity to not only finish paying off their consumer debt (which included a HELOC), they were also able to finish their emergency fund, and put a down payment on their dream home.

After they achieved financial freedom, they saved enough for Caleb to purchase his dream truck again. However, he realized his current truck did the job, so he decided to hold off on getting the dream truck so they could focus on other financial goals. He'll get his dream truck later. That is living with contentment. That is freedom.

FREEDOM HAS BEEN AVAILABLE ALL ALONG

Freedom has been available to you from the start. You were frozen in fear, unwilling to step onto the Awareness Level for so long, but once you brave the reality of your situation, you get your first taste of freedom. As you climb up the Pyramid, your hope and your confidence will grow with each level you complete until you reach the final peak—total financial freedom. You can do this! Let the hope charge you forward, feel the chains break and the burdens lift as you experience one victory after the other. Fear is gone, freedom is here.

Chapter 12 Takeaways

- **Hope in awareness.** You have faith in the future because now you know where you're at in your finances, and you've written down your goals.

- **Hope in knowledge.** There's no fear that your decisions will continue to set you back, to perpetuate your paycheck-to-paycheck prison, and to leave you stressed and overwhelmed. On the Knowledge Level, you know where you're going. This how-to map will get you there.

- **Hope in commitment.** Now you get to see the real fruit of your actions. On the Commitment Level, you buckle down and do what needs to be done to get through the Pyramid fast.

- **Hope in momentum.** Once you step onto the Momentum Level, hope compounds. One victory rolls into another victory as you knock down debt. That snowball effect is real and as your goals come closer, the reality of freedom becomes clearer and clearer.

- **Hope in freedom.** True freedom does come. The Freedom Level gives you an incredible amount of satisfaction, confidence, and peace. You did it! You achieved financial freedom!

- **Hope in accountability.** Accountability bridges the gap between knowledge and commitment. You'll be less likely to fall back into the Cycle of Regret with accountability.

CHAPTER 13

What's Next?

If you live like no one else, later you get to live and give like no one else.

—*Dave Ramsey*

WHEN YOU FINALLY REACH the top of the Financial Freedom Pyramid, you've completed Baby Step 3, which means you've saved three to six months of living expenses in your fully funded emergency fund and have no debt aside from your house. Sounds like a perfect scenario, doesn't it? Long before my clients cross this finish line, they relax, unclench their teeth, and release the breath they've been holding for years. This can be you. Getting out of debt gets you to some incredible places. No more money stress and fears. No more failure with finances. All by getting some discipline and living out a plan in line with God's best for your life. I'm cheering you on. I want your back-breaking sprint to financial freedom to be over.

But once you get there, you might ask, "What's next?" Well, there's saving for the down payment of your first house, saving for retirement, saving for your kids' future education, and paying off the house while building wealth and giving generously along the way. All of which would have seemed like an utter impossibility before you followed the Pyramid, right? But now you have the tools to accomplish all of it. You have the tools to set your whole family up for long-term financial success, to treat yourself to vacations, home improvements, better vehicles, and even cheese balls—as long as it's in the budget. Whatever is next for you, budgeting still needs to be 100 percent part of your plan. Budgeting is a way of life for the rest of your life, no matter how wealthy you become.

KEEP THE SAME PRINCIPLES

In Chapter 11 we talked about how compromising your principles from situation to situation can stunt your progress. Well, the same thing can happen at the top of the Pyramid. Once you have room in your budget, it's easy to justify that car loan payment or those vacation installments because unlike before, you have no alarm bells saying, "Whoa! I can't afford that." Instead, you think, "I *can* afford that." Next thing you know, you're back to credit cards and personal loans. Soon enough, you'll be back in the Cycle of Regret. Don't let your newfound wealth turn you into a frivolous spender or a risky investor. Stay true to your plan and keep on budgeting. Remember, without action and principles, your money situation, like your kid's chaotic bedroom, will only get worse, never better. But you know that now.

Before I close and watch you set sail on this journey, I wanted to leave you with one last hopeful example: It was the final session for Cole and Jamie. When they started with me, things were as bad as they come. Cole had had an injury and was home on disability, unable to work. To make ends meet, his wife, Jamie, worked five jobs. Yes, five! And to make things worse, they were fighting every day about money. They were stressed, overwhelmed, and completely miserable. While moving through the Pyramid, they downsized their house and sold their rental property. They budgeted well, stayed on task, and kept me as an accountability coach the whole way through.

Soon, they were 100 percent debt-free with a fully funded emergency fund and a paid-for house in five years. After that, Jamie dropped back down to one job and Cole's health improved so much that he was about to return to work. The two of them had stopped fighting about money too. They had not one money argument since starting the plan.

I know I need to let go of my clients at some point, but it's always sad to see them go. A few minutes before the end of the last meeting, Jamie said in a shy, quiet tone, "Justin, can I ask you a question?"

"Of course," I said, a little confused by her seeming reluctance.

"Cole and I have been thinking... We would really like to go to Jamaica. We haven't been there in a long time. Do you think it's okay if we go to Jamaica? We'd pay for everything in cash... we have the margin."

I was so happy for them. A big grin filled my face, and I declared, "My homework for you is to go to Jamaica and have the time of your life!"

They went and had the time of their lives. In fact, their fourteen-day vacation was the best, most relaxing trip they ever had. They didn't have to stress about money one bit; they had true financial freedom. A layer of peace covered all aspects of their lives. When they first set out on their financial journey, they envisioned a picturesque scene of sand between their toes, wind in their hair, and tranquility. And because they stuck with their plan, they got to experience it for real... sand actually between their toes, wind actually in their hair, and tranquility actually in their minds. It's the true idyllic future we all hope for.

When I talked to them about it, Jamie said, "It was so wonderful and so relaxing. Last time we went years ago, we thought we had to use credit cards for everything—airplane tickets, motel, food—everything. We couldn't enjoy it at all. In fact, I kept thinking we needed to hurry and get back so I could get to work and pay off the trip. This time... time felt like it stood still, so we could soak up every minute."

YOU'RE IN CONTROL NOW

This is what I want for you. You can have the future you always dreamed of with just a few steps up the Pyramid. You've done harder things and been through greater trials. This is one thing you can control. This is one thing that shouldn't control you. Today, take that first step towards financial freedom and choose the path that leads to the life you want. I'm praying for you, I believe in you, and I want you to book your own trip to Jamaica—or wherever financial freedom leads you.

FINANCIAL FREEDOM
CHECKLIST

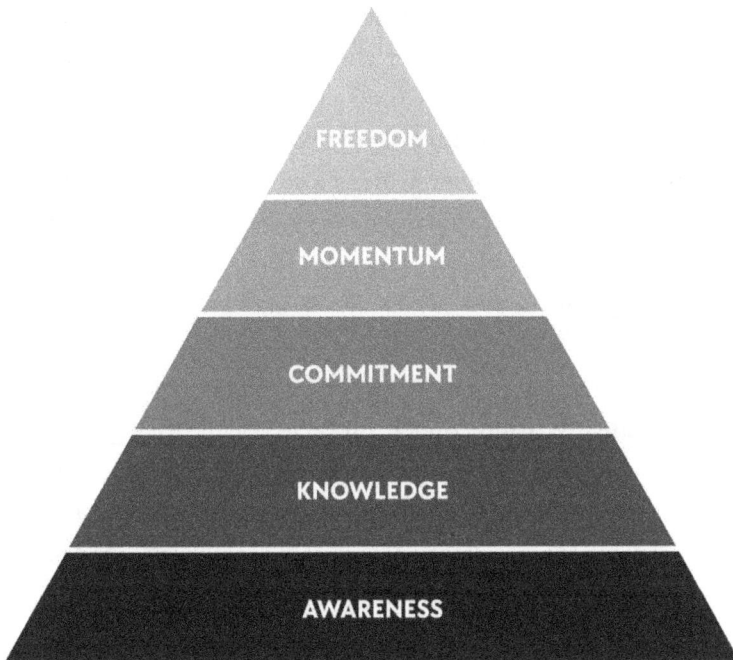

Awareness

Complete

☐ **Determine Household Income:** Write down where all your household income comes from. You'll want to use your take-home pay, the amount after all deductions and any benefits that come out of your check. You may want to reference paystubs and your bank account to get accurate numbers.

☐ **Determine All Monthly Expenses:** Write down all your expenses. This includes bills, debt payments, food, fuel, etc. Anything you spend money on needs to be recorded. Use a budget template to help ensure you do not leave any expenses out. You can also look at the last ninety days of bank statements.

☐ **Document Debt:** Write down who each of your creditors are, how much you owe for each debt, how much your minimum monthly payments are for each debt, and the interest rate for each one.

☐ **Establish Written Short-Term Goals:** Define what goals you want to accomplish during the first six months. Goals can include, but are not limited to, increasing savings, reducing debt, stopping paycheck-to-paycheck living, and being on the same page with your spouse. Be sure to include why each goal is important for you to reach.

☐ **Establish Written Long-Term Goals:** Define what goals you want to accomplish beyond six months. Goals can include, but are not limited to, becoming debt-free, saving a fully funded emergency fund, traveling, increasing generosity, investing for the future. Be sure to include why each goal is important for you to reach.

Level Up Your Awareness

Do you feel like you have no money left over at the end of the month? If you are struggling to find the margin you need to pay down debt faster and save for the future, a financial coach can help you gain clarity to know where all your money is going and to give you recommendations on what changes you can make to climb the financial freedom pyramid.

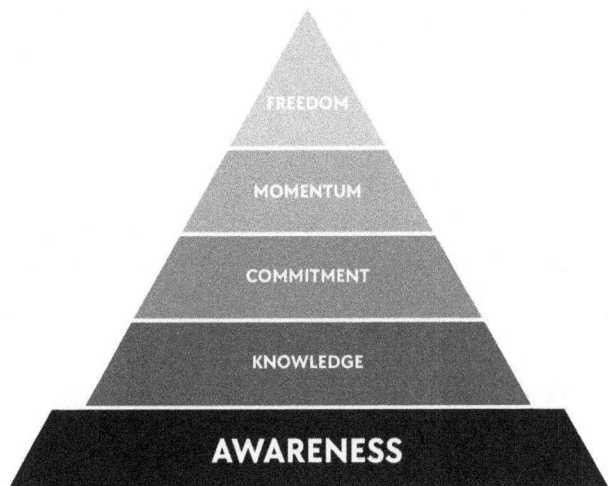

FREEDOM

MOMENTUM

COMMITMENT

KNOWLEDGE

AWARENESS

Knowledge

Complete

☐ **Live by the Seven Proven Biblical Principles:** To obtain financial freedom you need to have principles that you live by. Whether you believe in the Bible or not, these principles will guide you to financial freedom.

☐ **Follow Baby Steps 1 Through 3:** Use the first three Ramsey Baby Steps to pay off debt and build your fully funded emergency fund. Be sure to complete each step one at a time and in order.

☐ **Create First Budget:** Use the ten-step budgeting framework to complete your first budget. Remember, the first budget will not be perfect, and it takes ninety days on average to get the hang of budgeting.

☐ **Establish Cash System and Sinking Fund:** Determine which areas of your budget you'll use cash to help reduce impulse spending, and which non-monthly expenses you'll save for each month using the sinking-fund method.

☐ **Regular Communication:** If married, establish a weekly habit to meet for fifteen to thirty minutes to discuss and review your budget. After two or three months, you may go to meetings twice a month or once a month. If single, you'll want to find an accountability partner to meet at least monthly to hold you accountable to your goals.

Level Up Your Knowledge

Have you ever read a book, listened to a podcast, or attended a financial class or workshop and still struggled to make sense of why nothing seemed to work? This is where having a financial coach can help. They can sit down with you to help you gain understanding and explain the areas that are causing confusion and help remove the roadblocks to your success.

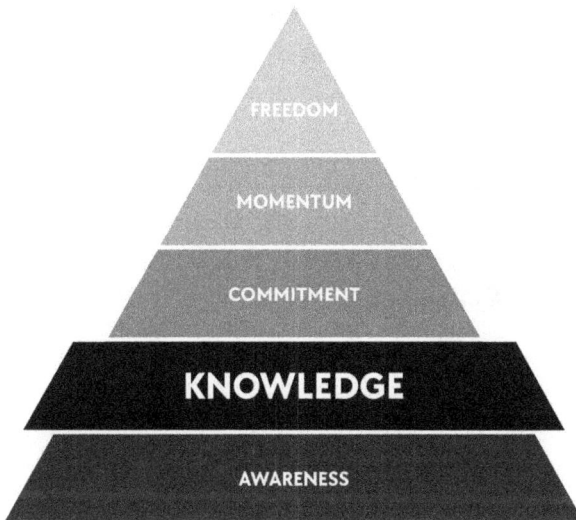

Commitment

Complete

☐ **Create New Budget Monthly:** Every month create a new budget before the month starts. After a few months of budgeting, you may not have to make many changes. Remember that your budget is not a set-it-and-forget-it tool.

☐ **Monthly Meeting Rhythm:** Continue a monthly discussion of your budget with your spouse, but consider meeting with a separate accountability partner or financial coach to maintain progress toward your goals.

☐ **Live Out Your Budget:** Stick to your budget that you have established. If something comes up you were not expecting, immediately update and balance your budget to reflect the change.

☐ **Cash Envelopes and Sinking Funds:** After each pay period, pull out cash for your envelope system and transfer money to your bank account for any non-monthly expenses you are saving for using the sinking-fund method.

☐ **Establish Debt Pay-Off Goal:** Determine when you're going to pay off all your debt (except your mortgage). Include how much extra per month from your budget will go towards debt elimination.

☐ **Don't Stop Being Accountable:** Meet with an accountability partner or financial coach at least once a month to maintain progress toward your goals.

Level Up Your Commitment

No longer is there a lack of awareness or knowledge holding you back—it's the lack of staying committed keeping financial freedom at bay. Change is hard, and you shouldn't go it alone. If you've tried before and failed, hiring a financial coach can hold you accountable to build the habits you need to win with money. Having someone to check-in with on your progress will help you take action, which will lead to results. Consistent results will level you up to Momentum, and you'll be one step closer to financial freedom.

Momentum

Complete

☐ **Live by Principles:** Stay the course by using the principles you have chosen to live by and avoid the four thieves that can S.L.O.W. down your momentum to pay off debt.

☐ **Adopt a Gain Mindset:** Remind yourself it's more important how far you've come to achieve financial freedom than how far you have left to go.

☐ **Maintain Traction:** Continue to live on a monthly budget, communicate about your finances, and pay extra to debt to reach your debt-free date.

☐ **Increase Traction:** Continually look for additional ways to pay off debt faster. Be creative. Make it a game. What additional expenses can you temporarily cut? What can you sell? How can you earn extra income?

☐ **Stretch Goal:** Each month, when you're close to paying off a debt, dig deep, and see what sacrifices you can make to pay off that debt one month earlier.

Level Up Your Momentum

If you're good at starting but something always seems to come up and derail you from hitting your goals, this is where you need to hire a coach. Hiring a coach can help you maintain and increase your traction while walking alongside you to help achieve financial freedom.

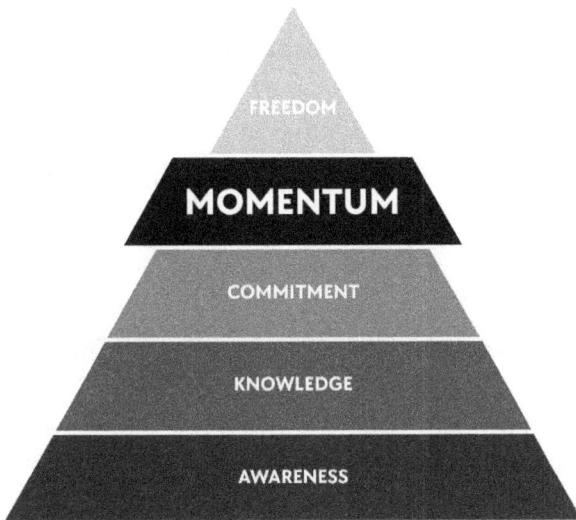

Freedom

Complete

☐ **Debt Free:** You did it! You have paid off all your consumer debt! Way to go!

☐ **Fully Funded Emergency Fund:** Take your $1,000 emergency fund and raise that amount to three to six months of living expenses.

☐ **Update Goals:** Review and update your goals. Now that you're out of debt and have a fully funded emergency fund, you may have new goals to add or new timelines for how long it will take you to reach some of your long-term goals you established earlier.

☐ **Budgeting Lifestyle:** Remember, budgeting is a way of life for the rest of your life. Now you can use your budget to accomplish financial goals like investing for the future, increasing generosity, and appropriately increasing budget categories to enjoy life.

☐ **Begin Financial Independence Journey:** Now that you have achieved financial freedom, you can focus on becoming financially independent. This is where wealth-building begins. Here you'll start the process of investing for retirement, saving for children's college (optional), and paying off your mortgage early.

Level Up Your Freedom

You did it! You reached financial freedom. If you're asking yourself the question, "What's next?" a financial coach can discuss what investing in your future looks like without selling any investment or insurance products. Yes, you will still need to hire a financial advisor to purchase your investments, but adding a financial coach creates a powerful one-two punch as you begin your journey to financial independence.

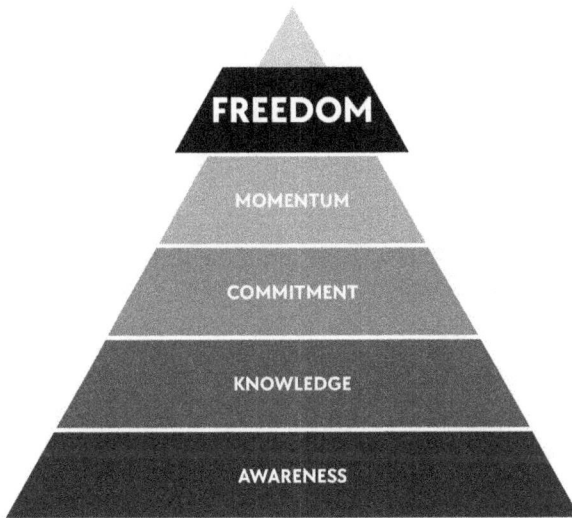

FREEDOM

MOMENTUM

COMMITMENT

KNOWLEDGE

AWARENESS

ACKNOWLEDGMENTS

FIRST, TO MY WIFE, JESSICA. Though I wrote the first draft myself, you had a hand in every version after that. Revision after revision, edit after edit, idea after idea, you were there to help inspire, encourage, course correct, and refine this book to what it is today. No one will truly know how much work you put in this book, and I cannot say thank you enough for pushing me to make *Level Up Your Finances* a reality.

To my editing team, Katie Gallardo, my developmental editor, who helped shape the rough gem of my manuscript, and Gleniece Lytle, my line editor, who refined and polished it to reveal what I pray will impact the financial lives of readers for generations to come.

To all those that gave me critical feedback on the book: Eva Daniels, Andrew Jay Lewis, Jacob Rains, Jada Rains, Julia Bennett, Jakob Riedell, Billie Shoemate, Ryan and Ashley Houck, Matt and Nancy Heerema, Emily Hawk, Craig Orman, Martin and Sherry Bracewell, Troy Jansen, Julia Mason, Bob Conroy, Greg Pare, Mark Lang, Marianne Renner, Tiffani Riedel, Callie Foster, Jordan Hall, David Foster, Trisha Staff, Brody Tritle, Kendra Oswald, Joe Bantz, Heidi Eickholt, Noha Plack, Angelica Torres, Irvin Sanchez, Kristine Stevenson, Darrell Bunting, Robbie Hyde, Lanessa Keehn, John Robertson, Jonathan Bracewell, Brian Myers, Gary Suddeth, and Jon Engelman.

A special thank you to authors AJ Harper and Mike Michalowicz. Mike's book, *Fix This Next*, was a great influence, and the week I started writing the first 20,000 words of this book, AJ's book, *Write a Must Read*, was announced. Later that year, their collaborative podcast, *Don't Write That Book*, launched. The timing was perfect for me, a first-time author. The wealth of knowledge you shared took this book to another level that never would have been a reality without you both. Thank you!

To Russ Carroll, Les Nienow, Lisa Barber, and Chris Hogan, without your training and guidance from the beginning, I would have never been the financial coach I am today.

Finally, Dave Ramsey, your passion and desire to help the masses get out of debt, build wealth, and become extremely generous infected me to the core. I remember the day I told you that someday I want to be doing what you are doing full-time. When you autographed my copy of your book, *The Total Money Makeover*, I asked you to write something inspiring. You wrote "Transform! Romans 12:2." Your frameworks not only transformed my family's finances forever, but you altered the trajectory of my career. I will be forever grateful for all the wisdom I have learned from you and your team.

Endnotes

INTRODUCTION

1. Erica Sweeney, "Most Americans Living Paycheck to Paycheck This Year, Survey Finds," Investopedia, September 18, 2023, https://www.investopedia.com/most-americans-report-living-paycheck-to-paycheck-new-survey-finds-7970611.

2. Ramsey, Financial Peace University [online course], Ramsey Store, Ramsey Solutions, accessed July 11, 2024, https://store.ramseysolutions.com/money/financial-peace-university/financial-peace-university.

3. Ramsey, "The 7 Baby Steps," Ramsey Solutions, Accessed on July 8, 2024, https://www.ramseysolutions.com/dave-ramsey-7-baby-steps.

CHAPTER 1

1. Kris Borghesan, "Americans Are Struggling Financially: 13 Financial Statistics You Need to Know," Savology, accessed July 9, 2023, https://savology.com/13-financial-statistics-you-need-to-know.

2. "Household Debt And Credit Report (Q2, 2024)," Center for Microeconomic Data, Federal Reserve Bank of New York, accessed September 19, 2024, https://www.newyorkfed.org/microeconomics/hhdc.

3. USAFacts Team, "Nearly half of American households have no retirement savings," USAFacts, last modified November 9, 2023, https://usafacts.org/data-projects/retirement-savings.

4. Poonkulali Thangavelu, "Survey: More cardholders carrying balances, credit card debt," Credit Cards, Bankrate, January 8, 2024, https://www.bankrate.com/finance/credit-cards/credit-card-debt-survey/.

5. Melanie Hanson, "Average Student Loan Debt," Education Data Initiative, last modified May 22, 2023, https://educationdata.org/average-student-loan-debt.

6. Rebecca Betterton, "Average car payments in 2024: What to expect," Auto Loans, Bankrate, May 31, 2024, https://www.bankrate.com/loans/auto-loans/average-monthly-car-payment/.

7. John Creamer and Matt Unrath, "End of Pandemic-Era Expanded Federal Tax Programs Results in Lower Income, Higher Poverty," United States Census Bureau, September 12, 2023, https://www.census.gov/library/stories/2023/09/median-household-income.html.

8. Andrew Dehan, "Average monthly mortgage payment," Mortgages, Bankrate, https://www.bankrate.com/mortgages/average-monthly-mortgage-payment/.

9. "USDA Food Plans: Monthly Cost of Food Reports," USDA Food and Nutrition Services, U.S. Department of Agriculture, accessed July 9, 2024, https://www.fns.usda.gov/cnpp/usda-food-plans-cost-food-monthly-reports.

10. "Composition of consumer unit: Annual expenditure means, shares, standard errors, and relative standard errors," PDF, Consumer Expenditure Surveys, U.S. Bureau of Labor Statistics, September, 2023, Table 1502, accessed July 9, 2024, https://www.bls.gov/cex/tables/calendar-year/mean-item-share-average-standard-error/cu-composition-2022.pdf.

11. "Americans spend $179 on fuel each month—here's how to spend less," CoPilit, January 18, 2023, https://www.copilotsearch.com/posts/americans-spend-179-on-fuel-each-month-how-to-spend-less/.

12. Maggie Davis, "Average Monthly Debt Payments Reach Nearly $1,600," LendingTree, January 22, 2024, https://www.lendingtree.com/personal/average-monthly-debt-payments-throughout-us/.

13. Maggie Davis, "Average Monthly Debt Payments Reach Nearly $1,600," LendingTree, January 22, 2024.

14. Maggie Davis, "Average Monthly Debt Payments Reach Nearly $1,600," LendingTree, January 22, 2024.

15. Taelor Candiloro, "Utility Bills 101: Average Costs of Utility Bills by State (2024 Guide)," Updated May 2, 2024, https://www.thisoldhouse.com/home-finances/reviews/utility-bills-101.

16. Ruben Caginalp and Mia Taylor, "Average cost of utility bills," Mortgages, Bankrate, November 16, 2023, https://www.bankrate.com/mortgages/average-utility-bills/.

17. Bobbi Dempsey, "Internet Service Provider Cost and Speed Survey," U.S. News & World Report, April 2, 2024, https://www.usnews.com/360-reviews/services/internet-providers/isp-cost-speed-survey-report.

18. Shannon Martin, "Average cost of car insurance in July 2024," Insurance, Bankrate, July 1, 2024, https://www.bankrate.com/insurance/car/average-cost-of-car-insurance/.

19. Bailey Schulz, "Subscription fatigue: More companies are charging monthly fees. How much can consumers take?," Money, USA Today, last modified February 22, 2023, https://www.usatoday.com/story/money/2023/02/22/monthy-subscription-fees-tiring-out-consumers/11313797002/.

20. "Consumer Expenditures—2022," News Release, Bureau of Labor Statistics, U.S. Department of Labor, September 8, 2023, https://www.bls.gov/news.release/pdf/cesan.pdf.

CHAPTER 2

1. Earl Nightingale, *The Strangest Secret: Essence of Success*, (Hawthorne, CA: BN Publishing, 2006).

2. Michael Hyatt, "5 Reasons Why You Should Commit Your Goals to Writing," Full Focus, accessed August 30, 2024, https://fullfocus.co/5-reasons-why-you-should-commit-your-goals-to-writing/.

3. Jim Rohn, Quotable Quotes, Goodreads, accessed on August 31, 2024, https://www.goodreads.com/quotes/855377-the-bigger-the-why-the-easier-the-how.

4. Michael Hyatt, "5 Reasons Why You Should Commit Your Goals to Writing," Full Focus, accessed August 30, 2024, https://fullfocus.co/5-reasons-why-you-should-commit-your-goals-to-writing/.

5. Phil McGraw Quotes. BrainyQuote.com, BrainyMedia Inc, accessed July 8, 2024, https://www.brainyquote.com/quotes/phil_mcgraw_204603.

6. Ken Coleman, The Ken Coleman Show (podcast), accessed October 9, 2024, https://www.ramseysolutions.com/shows/the-ken-coleman-show.

CHAPTER 3

1. The inspiration for this chapter comes from my attendance of Dave Ramsey's Financial Coach Master Training (formerly known as Dave Ramsey Counselor Training) in 2010.

2. The Ascent staff, "Study: It Pays to Be Generous," The Ascent, last modified October 27, 2021, https://www.fool.com/the-ascent/research/study-it-pays-be-generous.

3. Brett Beasley, "It (literally) pays to be generous," Notre Dame Deloitte Center for Ethical Leadership, accessed July 11, 2024, https://ethicalleadership.nd.edu/news/it-pays-to-be-generous/.

4. Ramsey, "Millionaire Spending Habits That Will Surprise You," Ramsey Solutions, January 13, 2022, https://www.ramseysolutions.com/budgeting/millionaire-spending-habits.

5. Chris Horymski, "Experian Study: Average U.S. Consumer Debt and Statistics," Experian, February 14, 2024, https://www.experian.com/blogs/ask-experian/research/consumer-debt-study/.

6. Alexandria White, "90% of Americans say money impacts their stress level, according to survey," CNBC Select, May 1, 2024, https://www.cnbc.com/select/why-americans-are-stressed-about-money/.

7. Dr. Thomas J. Stanley, *The Millionaire Mind*, (Kansas City: Andrews McMeel Publishers, 2001), 1.

8. Summer Allen, Ph.D., "The Science of Generosity," PDF, Greater Good Science Center-UC Berkeley, May 2018, https://ggsc.berkeley.edu/images/uploads/GGSC-JTF_White_Paper-Generosity-FINAL.pdf.

9. Sofie Isenberg, "Want To Feel Happier? Science Says Try Being More Generous," WBUR Kind World, Podcast, July 28, 2020, https://www.wbur.org/kindworld/2020/07/28/dunn-interview.

10. K. Eriksson, et al., "Generosity Pays: Selfish People Have Fewer Children and Earn Less Money," Journal of Personality and Social Psychology, PDF, accessed July 11, 2024, http://www.diva-portal.org/smash/get/diva2:1253120/FULLTEXT01.pdf.

11. Randy Alcorn, *Managing God's Money: A Biblical Guide*, (Tyndale House Publishers, 2011).

CHAPTER 4

1. Kris Borghesan, "Americans Are Struggling Financially: 13 Financial Statistics You Need to Know," Savology, accessed July 11, 2024, https://savology.com/13-financial-statistics-you-need-to-know.

2. Kris Borghesan, "Americans Are Struggling Financially: 13 Financial Statistics You Need to Know," Savology, accessed July 11, 2024.

3. Matt Schulz, "2024 Credit Card Debt Statistics," LendingTree, last modified July 8, 2024, https://www.lendingtree.com/credit-cards/credit-card-debt-statistics/.

4. Remi Trudel, "Research: The Best Strategy for Paying Off Credit Card Debt," Harvard Business Review, December 27, 2016, https://hbr.org/2016/12/research-the-best-strategy-for-paying-off-credit-card-debt.

CHAPTER 5

1. Rob Williams, "5 Ways Financial Planning Can Help," Charles Schwab, January 13, 2021, https://www.schwab.com/learn/story/5-ways-financial-planning-can-help.

2. Kris Borghesan, "Americans Are Struggling Financially: 13 Financial Statistics You Need to Know," Savology, accessed July 11, 2024, https://savology.com/13-financial-statistics-you-need-to-know.

3. *Shark Tank*, TV Series, S3.E13 aired May 4, 2012, IMDb, https://www.imdb.com/title/tt2374043/characters/nm1171860.

4. Rachel Telford, "Leading through change: Lessons from the 2017 March Classic," Ontario Grain Farmer Magazine, June 2017, https://ontariograinfarmer.ca/2017/06/01/leading-through-change/.

5. "Four Things to Talk About Before Marriage," FoundationsU, accessed on August 21, 2024, https://www.foundationsu.com/college/articles/foundationsu-four-things-to-talk-about-before-marriage.

CHAPTER 6

1. Google, accessed September 30, 2024, "Budget billing is a service that some utility companies offer to help customers pay their energy bills more consistently. It works by dividing the total amount spent on energy over the previous year by 12 to calculate a monthly payment amount. This results in a more predictable bill that's less affected by seasonal changes in energy usage."

2. Erin Hurd, "Does Using a Credit Card Make You Spend More Money?," NerdWallet, last modified May 28, 2024, https://www.nerdwallet.com/article/credit-cards/credit-cards-make-you-spend-more.

CHAPTER 7

1. Laine Gillespie, "Survey: More than 1 in 3 Americans earn money through side hustles, 32% think they'll always need them," Bankrate, July 10, 2024, https://www.bankrate.com/credit-cards/news/side-hustles-survey/#bankrate-s-insights-on-side-hustles.

2. Bailey Schulz, "Subscription fatigue: More companies are charging monthly fees. How much can consumers take?," Money, USA Today, last modified February 22, 2023, https://www.usatoday.com/story/money/2023/02/22/monthy-subscription-fees-tiring-out-consumers/11313797002/.

3. "The Diner Dispatch: 2023 American Dining Habits," US Foods, accessed July 11, 2024, https://www.usfoods.com/our-services/business-trends/american-dining-out-habits-2023.html.

4. Mike Rowe, *Dirty Jobs*, TV Series, 2005–2023, https://www.imdb.com/title/tt0458259/.

CHAPTER 8

1. John C. Maxwell, *The Maxwell Daily Reader: 365 Days of Insight to Develop the Leader Within You and Influence Those Around You*, (HarperCollins Leadership, 2011), quote from December 1 entry.

2. Dan Sullivan, *10X is Easier Than 2X: How World-Class Entrepreneurs Achieve More by Doing Less* (Carlsbad, CA: Hay House Business, 2023).

3. Gloria Guzman and Melissa Kollar, "Income in the United States: 2022," United States Census Bureau, September 12, 2023, https://www.census.gov/library/publications/2023/demo/p60-279.html#:~:text=Highlights,and%20Table%20A%2D1.

4. Zig Ziglar Quotes, QuoteFancy, quotefancy.com, accessed July 8, 2024, https://quotefancy.com/quote/943253/Zig-Ziglar-If-you-wait-until-all-the-lights-are-green-before-you-leave-home-you-ll-never.

CHAPTER 9

1. Steven Newland, "The Power of Accountability," The Standard Newsletter, Association for Financial Counseling & Planning Education, third quarter 2018, https://www.afcpe.org/news-and-publications/the-standard/2018-3/the-power-of-accountability/.

CHAPTER 10

1. Mike Michalowicz, *Clockwork, Revised and Expanded: Design Your Business to Run Itself*, (New York: Portfolio, 2022).

2. Rainey, Adrian. Quoted by Dan Sullivan, *10X is Easier Than 2X: How World-Class Entrepreneurs Achieve More by Doing Less* (Carlsbad, CA: Hay House Business, 2023).

CHAPTER 11

1. Keith Barry, "New Cars Aren't Always More Reliable, Despite What Buyers Think," Consumer Reports, June 28, 2018, https://www.consumerreports.org/cars/buying-a-car/new-cars-arent-always-more-reliable-survey-a1097859269/.

2. Dan Sullivan, *The Gap and the Gain: The High Achievers' Guide to Happiness, Confidence, and Success*, (Carlsbad, CA: Hay House Business, 2021).

CHAPTER 12

1. "You'll be 95% More Successful With This One Simple Leadership Trick," StellaPop, accessed July 11, 2024, https://stellapop.com/youll-be-95-more-successful-with-this-one-simple-leadership-trick/.

ABOUT THE AUTHOR

BY AGE TWENTY-FIVE, Justin was living the American Dream—or so he thought. But at the start of a promising banking career and after purchasing his first home with his wife, Jessica, their dream came crashing down. Overdrawn and anxious every month, and with over $100,000 in consumer debt, not counting their house, Justin was determined to learn sound financial principles that would take him from living paycheck to paycheck to gaining financial freedom. And he did. *Level Up Your Finances* is the framework for reaching that freedom.

For almost two decades, through his business, Strong Tower Consulting, Justin has coached over one thousand clients to gain control of their money and pay off a combined debt total of over ten million dollars.

Justin is a lifelong Iowan who enjoys smoking meats, playing the guitar, cycling, basketball, golfing, bowling, fishing, and sitting down to a good board game or game of cards. But most importantly, he loves spending time with his family. Justin has been married for over twenty years to his beautiful wife, Jessica. They have five children, a daughter-in-law, and one grandchild.

CUSTOMIZED COACHING PLANS

The accountability you need for success!

HIRE JUSTIN TO BE YOUR COACH!

INCREASE SAVINGS

ELIMINATE DEBT

DEVELOP A PLAN

CONTROL SPENDING

BECOME EMPOWERED

BE MOTIVATED TO START

CREATE A BUDGET

CONNECT WITH SPOUSE

GAIN FREEDOM

Contact: justin@levelupyourfinances.com

LEVEL UP YOUR FINANCES

MAKES A GREAT GIFT
FOR SOMEONE...

- 🎓 **Graduating**

- 💍 **Engaged**

- 💍 **Newlywed**

- ❤️ **You Care For**

- 📦 **Winging it With Money**

LEVEL UP YOUR FINANCES

IS A GREAT TOOL FOR:

- ✓ **Therapists**
- ✓ **Counselors**
- ✓ **Pastors**
- ✓ **Coaches**
- ✓ **Financial Professionals**

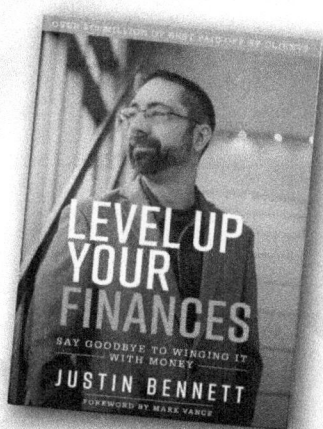

BUY THE BOOK HERE!
LevelUpYourFinances.com